Citizen's Guide to U.S. Foreign Policy Issues: Election '96

Nonpartisan briefs on key issues facing the nation

★ ★ ★

Prepared by the Editors
of the Foreign Policy Association

All rights reserved. No part of this book may be reproduced or transmitted in any form or by any means, electronic or mechanical, including photocopying, recording or by any informational storage and retrieval system, without permission in writing from the publisher.

Researched as of June 30, 1996.

Published by the Foreign Policy Association
Chairman: Paul B. Ford, Jr.
President: Noel V. Lateef
Editor in Chief: Nancy Hoepli-Phalon
Senior Editors: Ann R. Monjo and K.M. Rohan
Associate Editor: June Lee
Contributing Editors:
    Babken V. Babajanian, June Lee, Jacqueline Mazza, David C. Morrison, K.M. Rohan, Scott C. Thompson and ACCESS: A Security Information Service
Editorial Interns:
    Kirsten Ek, A. Dwayne Linville and Jane H. Yoon

Typography and design: K.M. Rohan

© Copyright 1996 by the Foreign Policy Association, Inc.
470 Park Avenue South, New York, N.Y. 10016-6819
Tel. (212) 481-8100; Fax. (212) 481-9275

Printed in the United States of America
Library of Congress Card Number: 96-85549
ISBN: 0-87124-171-4

Table of Contents

Introduction 5

HOT SPOTS

1. U.S. Role in the World 7
2. Bosnia and Herzegovina 17
3. China, Taiwan, Hong Kong 28
4. Russia 40
5. Mexico 52

HOT ISSUES

6. Middle East 62
7. Immigration 74
8. Trade and the Economy 84
9. U.S. Role in the UN 94
10. Defense and Security 103
11. Foreign Aid 112

    Index 121
    Order form 127

Introduction

PRESIDENT Franklin Delano Roosevelt wrote in 1943: *"In a democracy the Government functions with the consent of the whole people. The latter must be guided by the facts. The Foreign Policy Association is performing a high duty in facilitating the lucid presentation of the facts of world problems and their impact upon the United States."*

President Roosevelt's words are especially germane in today's hypermobile world, where international transfers of materials, information, capital and people are accelerating. The "whole people" is an inclusive constituency that must have access to both timely information and national deliberative processes in order to sustain democracy.

Citizens who understand the global issues affecting their lives, who form opinions and effectively express them, contribute to a strong democracy. Indeed, democracy demands knowledge and vision of its citizens no less than of its leaders. In the words of President James Madison: *"Knowledge will forever govern ignorance. And a people who mean to be their own governors must arm themselves with the power that knowledge gives."*

Foreign policy provides a lens for viewing our own society. Our willingness to confront aggressors, to aid those in dire need and to promote democracy worldwide are expressions of those values that define our society. In making the great decisions of foreign policy, we preserve or destroy those values accepted by our society as fundamental.

Defining a new vision of America's place in the world has been deferred under the assumption that we can prioritize between domestic and foreign policy. They are in fact inextricably linked. The appropriate level of defense spending and trade policy are illustrative of the seamless quality of the domestic/foreign policy continuum.

Unfortunately, the public does not follow international developments closely. A 1993 survey of eight democracies found American citizens dead last in their knowledge of current international events. More recently, U.S. Treasury Secretary Robert Rubin warned that there is "a desperate need for education at home about the importance of American engagement in the world."

The importance of this engagement is partly economic. Today, U.S. imports and exports amount to 30 percent of America's gross domestic product. However, prosperity and the "pursuit of happiness" presuppose a world at peace. As Yale University historian Donald Kagan reminds us: *"A persistent and repeated error through the ages has been the failure to understand that the preservation of peace requires effort, planning, the expenditure of resources, and sacrifice...."*

The world looks to the United States for leadership on many fronts. This presents a singular opportunity for the United States to shape a new global ethic steeped in democratic values.

In educating the public on vital international issues, the Foreign Policy Association (FPA) is driven by service to the nation and by the conviction, recently reaffirmed by former Federal Reserve Board Chairman Paul A. Volcker at an FPA forum, that any lasting success in international understanding depends on reaching a broader audience—an informed citizenry willing to support effective leaders.

We hope you will find this CITIZEN'S GUIDE useful, and we invite you to use it to frame questions that need to be asked of our elected representatives.

Noel V. Lateef
President

1

U.S. Role in the World

✔ *What role should the U.S. play in the world in the 21st century?*

✔ *Does the U.S. still need a large military establishment, and, if so, for what purposes?*

✔ *Does free trade best serve U.S. interests or should the U.S. seek to protect its industries and workers?*

✔ *What are the most important international issues facing the U.S. in the next four years?*

Basic Facts

- With almost 264 million people, the U.S. is the world's third most populated country. China with 1.2 billion people has the largest population, and India is second with 937 million.
- The U.S. has the world's largest economy, with a gross domestic product (GDP) of $7.25 trillion in 1995. Japan, with a GDP of $4.49 trillion, is second.
- The U.S. is the world's second-richest nation, with a per capita income of $27,530 (1995). Japan, with a per capita income of $35,801 (1995), is first.

- The U.S. foreign aid budget for fiscal year (FY) 1996 is $12.8 billion—less than 1% of the federal budget and 0.15% of GDP.

- The U.S. spends more on its military than any other country. The Clinton Administration is requesting $243 billion for defense in FY 1997. Russia is second with military expenditures of $63 billion in 1995.

- The U.S. armed forces have 1.5 million men and women—one of the world's largest military establishments. China, with armed forces of 2.9 million, has the world's largest.

Background

The U.S. emerged from World War II a nuclear superpower in a world prostrated by the physical, economic and political devastation of war. Europe, the Soviet Union and East Asia were in ruins. There were vast numbers of refugees and displaced persons left homeless by war and the Nazi Holocaust. As the war came to a close, the U.S. and its allies shaped a vision of the world around several policy goals. The objectives included a system of free, nondiscriminatory global trade; foreign aid and investment to rebuild nations devastated by war; encouragement of stable, market-oriented, democratic governments; and the creation of and support for international bodies, in particular the United Nations, that potentially could address international problems.

The peace was fragile and the alliance that had included the Soviet Union in opposition to Nazi aggression broke down. The containment of communism became the overriding U.S. foreign policy objective. A worldwide system of alliances, such as the North Atlantic Treaty Organization (NATO), was created to provide collective security against the spread of communism. Democratic and Republican Administrations alike pursued the containment policy for some 45 years. That goal having been achieved, the U.S. now faces a different set of challenges.

Key Issues

Leadership, partnership, or withdrawal?

America, having shouldered the burden of leadership for 50 years, has problems at home. How should the U.S. balance the demands for American leadership abroad with the need for attention to domestic problems?

- ■ ***U.S. hegemony, or world leadership.*** With the collapse of the Soviet Union, the U.S. is the only economic and military superpower left in the world. Some Americans feel that this reality brings with it both the responsibility and the opportunity to shape the structure of the post-cold-war world. They feel that, having won the cold war, the U.S. should focus on protecting American interests and American leadership. Those who hold this view tend to support maintaining a strong U.S. military presence capable of intervening where U.S. interests are threatened. Some want the U.S. to take the lead in multilateral efforts that directly affect U.S. interests.

- ■ ***U.S. cooperative engagement, or partnership, in a changing world.*** Polling data indicates that most Americans prefer multilateral arrangements where the burden of dealing with global problems is shared by other nations. Those who favor this view see a complex multipolar world that requires the cooperation of many nations. They tend to believe the U.S. should work with

By Oliphant. Reprinted with permission of Universal Press Syndicate. All rights reserved.

other countries through multilateral organizations such as the UN, a restructured NATO, the Group of Seven (G-7) major industrialized democracies and other cooperative bodies. They tend to believe that the U.S. cannot afford to lead the post-cold-war world unilaterally, and wish to see other nations carry their share of the burden.

Some business leaders support a variation on this theme. They may favor U.S. support for free trade and for the spread of democratic capitalism, but at the same time they are opposed to the growth of bureaucracy, whether in the U.S. government or international agencies. Some also oppose what they view as excessive U.S. military spending and adventurism, and they would prefer to see taxes lowered and private investment increased.

■ *U.S. withdrawal, or come home America.* Some Americans believe that the U.S., which spent enormous sums in superpower competition with the Soviet Union, neglected its own infrastructure, cities, industry and citizens. They believe the U.S. needs to reduce international commitments of all kinds and put its own house in order. Some favor strictly limiting America's overseas commitments to regions where U.S. strategic interests are very clear, as in the Middle East. Some people also favor substantially reducing military spending, restricting immigration, cutting foreign aid and limiting free-trade agreements.

In the current U.S. policy debate on the question of U.S. leadership, traditional liberal and conservative positions are often mixed. Both liberal and conservative groups may oppose military actions such as the Persian Gulf war, but for very different reasons. Some internationalists who support strengthening the UN but oppose the use of military force may agonize over their position on a multilateral UN-approved military force in Somalia or Bosnia.

Military force

The U.S. has been reducing the size of the military and closing bases for several years. Even so, the U.S. spends far more on its military than any other nation. With no superpower threatening the U.S., and no strong

Harley Schwadron

enemies, does the U.S. need to maintain such a large military force? The U.S. Department of Defense recommends a military force structure capable of fighting two nearly simultaneous Persian Gulf–size wars without significant support from allies. (See Chapter 10, "Defense and Security.") This strategy would require maintaining or increasing U.S. military spending. Some critics believe it is unlikely that the U.S. would face such a scenario and argue that such expenditures are not needed. President Bill Clinton believes that further cuts in the defense budget are unwise and would have adverse effects on military readiness and on the U.S. economy. Republican presidential candidate and former Senate Majority Leader Bob Dole and some other Republicans believe that some increase in the defense budget may be necessary to pursue a ballistic-missile-defense capability and ensure an adequate force structure to protect American interests.

■ *Overseas troop commitments.* In recent years, the U.S. has been reducing its overseas troop commitments, especially in Western Europe. The U.S. and Japan recently signed an agreement that leaves American forces in Japan at approximately their present level, but increases Japan's commitments to its own defense. Many specialists believe that the U.S. has strategic interests in the Middle East, Western Europe and East Asia. These regions supply the U.S. with fuel and its strongest trading partners and allies. U.S. peacekeeping forces have been involved in multilateral humanitarian and peace missions in Somalia, Haiti, Rwanda, Macedonia and Bosnia, among others. U.S. policy has been criticized by some as ambiguous. Clinton has indicated that the U.S. would continue to commit troops when he felt the mission was achievable and well-defined. Dole supports limiting U.S. military participation to operations of clear strategic interest.

■ *Nuclear weapons.* At the cold war's end, the U.S. and Russia committed themselves to reducing their nuclear arsenals and ending the arms race. The U.S. helped Russia dismantle its nuclear stockpiles and worked with the newly independent states of Ukraine, Kazakhstan and Belarus to remove Soviet nuclear weapons on their territory. Despite progress on this front, and the indefinite extension in 1995 of the Nuclear Nonproliferation Treaty of 1968, most experts see a continuing threat to U.S. security. These experts fear the spread of missile technology and weapons-grade materials to states such as Pakistan and Iran, as well as the use of nuclear, chemical or biological weapons by terrorist states or groups. While many agree that weapons proliferation poses a threat, there is disagreement about how best to respond. Dole and many conservative Republicans argue that the uncertainties in Russia and the danger of proliferation make it dangerous for the U.S. to reduce too rapidly its nuclear arsenals. Others argue that it is important now to continue to reduce cold-war nuclear arsenals while the international political climate is favorable. These specialists fear that if the U.S. delays major reductions, the Russian military may renew the arms race.

Free trade vs. greater protection for American workers and business

By 1996, a series of trade negotiations conducted over several decades under the auspices of the General Agreement on Tariffs and Trade (GATT) had lowered trade barriers and opened up markets. Only a few small closed economies remain in the world (e.g., North

Korea's). Americans are now most concerned about their widening trade deficit, especially with Japan. The Clinton Administration has spearheaded an era of more-aggressive trade negotiations and government advocacy of U.S. exports. Both President Clinton and Dole support the North American Free Trade Agreement (Nafta), which they argue has increased trade and created new jobs. Critics of the agreement, primarily U.S. labor unions, charge that American workers need protection from low-wage nations such as Mexico to protect American jobs.

Attitudes of the American public

Recent opinion polls show an ambivalent attitude by the American public toward U.S. international involvement. In general, Americans remain committed to U.S. participation in the UN and other global concerns, but fear the U.S. is shouldering more than its share of the burden. Many believe that, at present, issues at home are more pressing than issues abroad.

Several surveys indicate that Americans prefer a multilateral approach to international crises and conflicts through the UN. A Times Mirror Center for the People and the Press poll in June 1995 showed that 13% of Americans wanted the U.S. to be "the single world leader" while 74% thought the U.S. should "play a shared leadership role." A series of polls in 1995 by the Program on International Policy Attitudes at the University of Maryland show that most Americans overestimate how much the U.S. is spending on peacekeeping and foreign aid, and they believe the U.S. is doing more than its share. At the same time, these polls show 76% of Americans believe "we should send aid to starving people irrespective of whether it will promote the national interest."

Administration Policy

The Clinton Administration has promoted a policy of supporting international institutions and relationships to strengthen multilateral approaches to world problems. The Administration committed American troops to Haiti to restore Jean-Bertrand Aristide to the presidency and remove a military dictatorship and it authorized sending U.S. troops as part of a NATO force to Bosnia. The Administration has also given priority to diplomatic efforts to encourage the development of peace in the Middle East. Clinton's highest priorities have been furthering global trade and promoting American competitiveness.

Regarding international organizations and foreign aid, the Administration has been opposed in Congress by critics of UN waste and mismanagement and by those who believe the U.S. should not send aid dollars abroad when programs for Americans are being cut back. Dole favors international engagement but criticizes Clinton for being too oriented toward multilateral approaches. He also criticizes Clinton for a policy of "indecision, vacillation and weakness [that] is making the world a more dangerous place" and leaves allies and opponents confused.

Policy Options

1. U.S. Role:

❏ **a.** The U.S. should exercise its leadership in the world to help shape the international framework for the 21st century.

OR

❏ **b.** The U.S. should focus on its own problems and let other nations carry the burden of leadership for a while.

2. Military Force:

❏ **a.** The U.S. still needs a large military force to keep it secure in a still-dangerous world.

OR

❏ **b.** The U.S. should sharply reduce military spending and shrink the defense bureaucracy.

3. Nuclear Weapons:

❏ **a.** The U.S. should pursue further reductions in the nuclear arsenals of the U.S. and Russia.

OR

❏ **b.** It is too soon to shrink a nuclear deterrent that protected America and its allies during the cold war.

4. **Free Trade:**
- ❏ a. The U.S. should continue to support free trade to expand U.S. markets.
    OR
- ❏ b. The U.S. should concentrate on protecting American workers and industries impacted by global trade.

5. **Foreign Aid:**
- ❏ a. The U.S. should continue to invest in building democracy, peace and free markets abroad.
    OR
- ❏ b. The U.S. should focus more on its domestic problems and let other nations take care of themselves.
    OR
- ❏ c. The U.S. can and must do both.

Select Bibliography

Chace, James, "New World Disorder?: U.S. in Search of a Role." *Great Decisions 1994*, pp. 83–90. New York, Foreign Policy Association, 1994. An essay by *World Policy Journal* editor who is also a professor at Bard College.

Hyland, William G., "A Mediocre Record," and Ullman, Richard H., "A Late Recovery." *Foreign Policy*, Winter 1995–96, pp. 69–80. Two experts give Clinton a "report card" on the conduct of his foreign policy.

Ikenberry, G. John, "The Myth of Post–Cold War Chaos." *Foreign Affairs*, May/June 1996, pp. 79–91. Rebuts claim that world order has changed.

Kull, Steven, "What the Public Knows that Washington Doesn't," and Rosner, Jeremy D., "The Know-Nothings Know Something." *Foreign Policy*, Winter 1995–96, pp. 102–29. Contrasting analyses of polling data on foreign policy concerns of the American public.

Mandelbaum, Michael, "Foreign Policy as Social Work." *Foreign Affairs*, Jan./Feb. 1996, pp. 16–32. Assessment of Clinton's foreign policy.

16 ■ U.S. Role

"A National Security Strategy of Engagement and Enlargement." The White House, Feb. 1996. 45 pp. Washington, D.C., Government Printing Office, Superintendent of Documents. Tel: (202) 512-1800. Outlines the Clinton Administration's national security strategy in a "radically transformed security environment."

2

Bosnia and Herzegovina

✔ *Should the U.S. extend its participation in the NATO force in Bosnia and Herzegovina beyond 1996?*

✔ *Should the U.S. help to rebuild the war-ravaged countries of the former Yugoslavia?*

✔ *Should NATO and UN forces help bring war criminals to justice?*

Basic Facts

- **The land:** During the war in Bosnia and Herzegovina that broke out in 1992, Bosnian Croats and Serbs sought to control the territory each seized in combat and create a new Bosnian nation made up of three ethnically based states. The Muslim-led Bosnian government sought to maintain Bosnia as a unified state. The surrounding states of Croatia and Serbia each supported their own ethnic group within Bosnia. Under the 1995 Dayton peace accords, Bosnia and Herzegovina is a confederation of two entities, the Bosnian Serb republic and the Muslim-Croat federation.
- **Pre-war population (July 1991):** 4,364,000: 44%

Muslim, 33% Serb, 17% Croat, 6% Other.
- **Leaders:** Bosnian President Alija Izetbegovic; Bosnian Serb leader Radovan Karadzic; Bosnian Croat leader Mate Boban; Serbian President Slobodan Milosevic; Croatian President Franjo Tudjman.
- **Military forces:** U.S. troops are participating in a multinational NATO peacekeeping force in Bosnia. There are 20,000 U.S. forces in Bosnia, and another 15,000 U.S. forces nearby in Croatia, Hungary and the Adriatic.
- **Casualties:** War in the former Yugoslavia has resulted in a quarter of a million dead and nearly 3 million refugees—the highest toll in Europe since World War II.
- **Aid:** Bosnia and Herzegovina has been promised $1.8 billion by the World Bank and other donors in reconstruction aid for 1996.

Background

Like the rest of the Balkans, Bosnia and Herzegovina has been fought over by peoples from many different cultures. In the sixth century, Slavs established settlements in this region. From that point on, Bosnia saw Roman Catholics and followers of Eastern Orthodoxy and Islam move into the region. In the late 15th century, the Ottoman Empire conquered this region and its rule lasted until World War I.

After World War I and the collapse of the Ottoman and Austro-Hungarian empires in 1918, Bosnia and Herzegovina became part of the Kingdom of Serbs, Croats and Slovenes. The name was changed in 1929 to Yugoslavia. The multiethnic makeup of the new country contributed to a power struggle between Croats and Serbs. In World War II, a Nazi Croatian puppet regime carried out a campaign of genocide against Serbs, Jews and Gypsies. Serbs in the region have not forgotten these massacres.

Bosnia and Herzegovina became a constitutional republic of the Yugoslav federation after World War II. (The other members of the federation were Serbia,

Croatia, Slovenia, Montenegro and Macedonia.) In 1971, Yugoslav President Marshal Josip Broz Tito established the Slavic Muslim minority as a distinct ethnic group in Yugoslavia as part of his plan to balance Serb and Croat power in Yugoslavia. Tito's death in 1980 left Yugoslavia without a leader who could keep the country unified. Competing nationalisms among the different ethnic groups, aggravated by a leadership crisis, led to the breakup of the country.

In June 1991, Croatia and Slovenia declared independence from Yugoslavia. War erupted in the two republics when the Serb leadership of Yugoslavia attempted to maintain the unity of the country by force. Uncomfortable with the increasing Serb drive for domination of Yugoslavia, Muslims and Croats in the Bosnia and Herzegovina parliament proposed that the republic declare independence from Yugoslavia. After the Bosnian Serbs walked out, Muslim and Croat legislators on October 15, 1991, declared Bosnia and Herzegovina a sovereign state with the same borders it had as a Yugoslav republic. The Bosnian Serbs rejected parliament's declaration and proclaimed loyalty to Yugoslavia. They formed an "Assembly of the Serb Nation" on October 24, 1991, led by Dr. Radovan Karadzic. A Bosnian Serb referendum in November resulted in a landslide vote in favor of remaining in the Yugoslav federation. The Bosnian Croats and Muslims also held a referendum, in early 1992, and 99.4% (minus most Bosnian Serbs who declined to participate) supported independence from Yugoslavia for Bosnia and Herzegovina.

On March 3, 1992, Bosnia and Herzegovina President Izetbegovic proclaimed the republic's independence. This was followed in April 1992 by international recognition of Bosnia and Herzegovina by the European Community and the United Nations. Troops from the Yugoslav army and Serbia invaded Bosnia and Herzegovina in an attempt to secure and consolidate Bosnian Serb territory. The war lasted until late 1995, when the Dayton peace accords, initialed by the presidents of Croatia, Serbia and Bosnia and Herzegovina on November 21, 1995, produced an uneasy settlement.

From the beginning, the Bosnian Serbs had the advantage because they received considerable support from Yugoslavia and had inherited most of the weapons and trained officer corps left in Bosnia and Herzegovina by the Yugoslav National Army. By contrast, the Bosnia and Herzegovina government forces, although superior in number, were poorly equipped and trained, and an arms embargo imposed by the UN in September 1991 prevented them from importing additional arms. As a result, the government's troops steadily lost ground to the Bosnian Serbs through the first year of the war. Thousands of Muslims, Croats and Serbs were forced from their homes by the fighting and became dependent on outside humanitarian aid. The largest Bosnian city, Sarajevo, and several regional urban areas were besieged.

A number of UN-brokered peace plans called for a division of the country along ethnic lines. The Bosnian government, committed to a Bosnian state with a Muslim majority, argued that such a division only rewarded Serb aggression. The Bosnian Serbs objected that the plans required them to give up substantial territory that they had won in battle. Divided opinion in the West, including U.S. criticism of the various peace proposals, contributed to their failure. Throughout the negotiations, numerous cease-fires were agreed to and almost immediately violated, usually by the Serbs.

The UN peacekeeping mission, Unprofor, was sent into the region in 1992. The only clear missions of Unprofor, the delivery of humanitarian aid and escort of refugees, were conducted under hazardous conditions with continual interference by all sides, especially the Bosnian Serbs. Western leaders did not want to become entangled in Bosnia but were compelled by public demand to do something to take a moral stand and end the violence.

In April 1993, the UN declared Operation Deny Flight, imposing a no-fly zone over Bosnia to be enforced by the North Atlantic Treaty Organization (NATO). It also declared six "safe areas" in Muslim-controlled Bosnia (Sarajevo, Bihac, Tuzla, Zepa, Srebrenica and Gorazde), partially to stem the flow of refugees to the West. The Serbs continued to subject these safe areas to artillery and sniper fire, while the Bosnian army used them as bases for military operations.

The military effectiveness of the Bosnian government's army slowly improved as a trickle of arms (mostly from Muslim countries such as Saudi Arabia and Iran) arrived in Bosnia with the tacit support of the U.S. In October 1994, the Bosnian government took Bihac, a UN safe area, with Croat assistance, and the Serbs responded with a fierce counterattack. NATO defended Bihac by bombing the Serbs. In spring 1995, NATO escalated its air campaign by bombing Serb ammunition dumps. The Serbs responded by taking UN peacekeepers hostage and using them as human shields. The hostages were eventually released. In July, however, the Serbs overran the UN safe area of Srebrenica. Bosnian Serb Gen. Ratko Mladic appeared in person to assure the civilians and the media that all Muslims would be safely conducted out of danger. It is alleged that shortly thereafter there was a mass execution of thousands of military-age Muslim men. Zepa was taken by the Bosnian Serbs on July 25, 1995. NATO responded by threatening to bomb the Serbs to protect the remaining three safe areas. In August and September, NATO launched an intensive campaign of air strikes against the Serbs.

In August, the Croatian army launched an offensive against the Serbs in Krajina, a region of Croatia that had been taken by Serbs in 1991. Serbian President Milosevic offered the Croatian Serbs no support and they were overwhelmed. Nearly 200,000 Croat refugees fled into Bosnia. Croatian forces carried out many atrocities. The successful offensive shifted the balance of power in the region away from the Serbs.

A split developed between Milosevic, who was becoming more amenable to a peace settlement, and the Serbs in Bosnia, particularly Bosnian Serb leader Karadzic, a potential political rival. Serbia was suffering greatly as a result of the UN economic sanctions imposed in May 1992.

Dayton peace accords

During the early fall of 1995, U.S. Assistant Secretary of State Richard C. Holbrooke began a period of round-the-clock shuttle-diplomacy negotiations with all the Bosnian factions, Croatia and Serbia. This produced a tenuous cease-fire in October, and paved the way for the peace talks in Dayton, Ohio, which began on November 1.

The Dayton peace accords, which were signed in Paris on December 14, 1995, maintained a single Bosnia and Herzegovina but divided it into two roughly equal parts: the Muslim-Croat federation, occupying 51% of Bosnian territory, and a Serb republic, receiving the remaining 49% of Bosnia. Some territory was to be transferred between the federation and the Serbs. Sarajevo was to be reunited, under predominantly Muslim control. Transfers of territory are occurring, accompanied by the destruction of properties left behind for the enemy. (Analysts predict that the Bosnian Serbs will eventually confederate with Yugoslavia, now composed of only Serbia and Montenegro, and the Muslim-Croat federation will join Croatia proper.) The agreement also had provisions for arms control, free elections, return of prisoners of war (POWs) and an accounting for prisoners, departure of all foreign forces, free movement of persons (including the right of refugees to return to their homes), cooperation with the International War Crimes Tribunal, military demobilization and the writing of a new constitution.

The agreement calls for a zone of separation to be set up between the Muslim-Croat federation and the Serb republic. This zone is being enforced by troops from the Implementation Force (IFOR), NATO's peacekeeping arm. Unlike the UN peacekeepers, IFOR has much more discretion in the use of force for self-defense, and more importantly, includes 20,000 American troops. IFOR will remain in place for one year. It is unclear who will take on IFOR's mission if further peacekeeping is required.

In related agreements, the only remaining Serb-occupied part of Croatia, Eastern Slavonia, will be returned to the control of the Croatian government following demilitarization and a period of international administration.

War crimes

Throughout the conflict, all three sides have been accused of practicing "ethnic cleansing" in territory they control. This action, to make a region ethnically homogeneous, includes murder, rape and the forced expulsion of individuals from their homes and property. Throughout the conflict, different ethnic groups have been accused of committing atrocities, though the Serbs are widely regarded as the worst offenders.

The UN Security Council established an International War Crimes Tribunal in May 1993 to prosecute war criminals in the former Yugoslavia. The chief prosecutor, South African judge Richard Goldstone, has issued more than 55 indictments since November 1994, mostly against Bosnian Serbs (including Karadzic and Ratko Mladic), but also against a few Muslims and Croats. The tribunal is hamstrung by its lack of an enforcement mechanism; there is no means of apprehending the war criminals under indictment who are still in the former Yugoslavia. Thus far, only one defendant has been taken into custody, and he was arrested in Germany while hiding from his superiors. In January

1996, U.S. Secretary of Defense William J. Perry promised to assist the tribunal's work with intelligence information and security.

The issue of war crimes is increasingly important within the region. Victims of atrocities seek justice from the international tribunal and information about those who have disappeared and are feared dead. Bosnian Serbs, however, charge that the tribunal is biased and thus far have refused to give up Karadzic and Mladic for trial.

Many journalists on the scene have been horrified by the concentration camps, genocide and wartime atrocities in Bosnia and Herzegovina. But American society remains divided between wishing to prevent another Holocaust and fearing entrapment in the quagmire of another Vietnam.

Administration Policy

When the conflict began in 1991, President George Bush opposed U.S. involvement. The U.S. had just concluded the Persian Gulf war and Bush was under sharp criticism in the U.S. for devoting too much attention to foreign policy. With an election year coming up, Bush preferred that the war in Yugoslavia be dealt with by the European Union and the Organization for Security and Cooperation in Europe; later by the UN. Under criticism from his election opponent, Bill Clinton, Bush became more involved with Bosnia and Herzegovina, beginning with backing UN Security Council Resolution 770, authorizing the use of force to ensure the delivery of humanitarian aid.

Clinton made Bosnia and Herzegovina an election issue in 1992. He originally favored lifting the arms embargo on Bosnia, arguing that it denied Bosnians the right to self-defense and froze the Serb's military advantage, and using NATO air power to protect Unprofor (the so-called "lift-and-strike" policy). France and Britain, with substantial troop contributions to Unprofor, complained that the U.S. was advocating stronger measures that put other countries' troops at risk but was itself unwilling to risk U.S. ground troops. Partially in response to European criticism, Clinton promised to supply American troops in support of a peace agreement and to aid in the withdrawal of Unprofor, should that become necessary. Clinton later reversed his stance on the lifting of the arms embargo on Bosnia, stating that it would alienate America's European allies.

Clinton's Republican opposition in the U.S. is split on Bosnia. Former Senate Majority Leader and Republican presidential candidate Bob Dole labeled the arms embargo a denial of Bosnia's right to self-defense and stated that lifting the embargo would "level the playing field" in Bosnia. Dole and other Republicans in Congress tried to attach a provision unilaterally lifting the arms embargo on Bosnia to the 1994 defense appropriations bill. It passed the House of Representatives but was voted down in the Senate 51 to 50 that summer, with Vice President Al Gore casting the tie-breaking vote. A second attempt in 1995 to lift the embargo unilaterally was passed by Congress but vetoed by Clinton. Republican support for arming and training the Bosnian Muslim army is also strong.

On the issue of U.S. troop deployment as part of IFOR, the Republican position is split. Dole, Senator John McCain (R-Ariz.) and other Republicans do not support the President's Bosnian policies nor the Dayton peace accords. However, they do support the participation of U.S. troops, yet call for conditions limiting their involvement. Others, among them Senator Phil

Danziger©*The Christian Science Monitor*

Gramm (R-Tex.), oppose the deployment of U.S. troops in Bosnia and Herzegovina because it risks a second Vietnam and is not sufficiently related to American national interests to risk the lives of U.S. soldiers.

Policy Options

1. **The U.S. should keep its troops in Bosnia and Herzegovina beyond the one-year deadline if necessary to enforce the Dayton peace accords.**

❏ **Yes.** Peace in the Balkans is a vital U.S. interest, and the U.S. must be prepared to provide continued leadership and troops for as long as necessary to secure the peace.

❏ **No.** The Balkans, the scene of bloody conflicts for centuries, are a European problem, and the U.S. has no clear strategic interests there. The U.S. should cease its military involvement and avoid a quagmire like Vietnam.

2. **The U.S. should assist the International War Crimes Tribunal by helping enforce arrest orders for war criminals.**

❏ **Yes.** The world has an obligation to bring war criminals to justice, and NATO forces including U.S. troops should help enforce the arrest orders of the war crimes tribunal.

❏ **No.** As terrible as the atrocities in Bosnia were, it is more important for NATO troops to implement the Dayton peace accords than to apprehend war criminals. The U.S. should continue to share intelligence but its troops should not make arrests which could reignite the war.

On the issue of aid to Bosnia and Herzegovina, see the chapter on foreign aid.

Select Bibliography

Freedman, Lawrence, "Why the West Failed." *Foreign Policy*, Winter 1994–95, pp. 53–69. How NATO missed its opportunity to ensure a "good" solution to the Bosnian conflict.

Rieff, David, "The Lessons of Bosnia: Morality and Power." *World Policy Journal*, Spring 1995, pp. 76–88. Evaluates efforts of the West during the Bosnian crisis.

"Securing a Peace Agreement for Bosnia." *U.S. Department of State Dispatch Supplement.* Dec. 1995. Remarks from President Bill Clinton, Secretary of State Warren Christopher and Deputy Secretary of State Strobe Talbott on the Dayton peace accords in Bosnia and Herzegovina. Includes fact sheets and a chronology.

Silber, Laura, and Little, Allan, *Yugoslavia: Death of a Nation.* New York, TV Books/Penguin USA, 1995. Argues the Serbian leadership "deliberately and systematically" killed Yugoslavia.

Woodward, Susan L., "Conflict in Former Yugoslavia: Quest for Solutions." *Great Decisions 1994*, pp. 3–14. New York, Foreign Policy Association, 1994. Senior fellow at the Brookings Institution provides historical analysis of the conflict in the Balkans and alternative policy options for the U.S.

3

China, Taiwan, Hong Kong

- ✔ *Does China's growing economic and military power pose a threat to the U.S.?*
- ✔ *Should the U.S. continue to grant China most-favored-nation trade status?*
- ✔ *How should the U.S. respond to China's human-rights violations?*
- ✔ *Should the U.S. defend Taiwan if China attacks it? Should the U.S. recognize Taiwan as an independent nation?*

Basic Facts

CHINA

Population:	1.2 billion (1995)
GNP per capita:	$490 (1993)*
GDP growth rate:	10.2% (1995)
U.S.-China trade:	$60 billion (1995)
U.S. balance of trade with China:	–$34 billion (1995)
Armed forces:	2.93 million active

*All figures in U.S. dollars.

TAIWAN

Population:	21.2 million (1995)
GNP per capita:	$12,000 (1995)*
GDP growth rate:	6% (3rd quarter, 1995)
U.S.-Taiwan trade:	$36.1 billion (1995)
U.S. balance of trade with Taiwan:	–$6.7 billion (1995)
China-Taiwan trade:	$18–$21 billion (1995)
Armed forces:	376,000 active

HONG KONG

Population:	6.3 million (1995)
GDP per capita:	$24,100 (1995)
GDP growth rate:	5.0% (1995)
U.S.-Hong Kong trade:	$18.2 billion (1995)
U.S. balance of trade with Hong Kong:	$3 billion (1995)
China-Hong Kong trade:	$127.6 billion (includes $49.7 billion of reexports) (1995)

*All figures in U.S. dollars.

Background

China

The People's Republic of China (PRC) was established October 1, 1949, after the Communist victory over the Nationalists in a civil war. Mao Zedong led China for 27 turbulent years until his death in 1976. Deng Xiaoping assumed the leadership in 1977 and led China down the road to market-based economic development. Market forces now determine most prices, state controls on industry have been loosened, and private enterprise and foreign investment are encouraged. For the last 14 years, China has experienced an unprecedented rate of growth—exceeding 9% a year. By the 1990s it had become the world's fastest-growing economy. China is the second-largest economy in East Asia, and, if Taiwan and Hong Kong are included, constitutes America's third-largest trading partner after Canada and Japan.

Economic liberalization, however, has not gone hand in hand with political liberalization. The PRC remains a repressive one-party state. The Chinese People's Liberation Army's violent crackdown on pro-democracy protesters in Tiananmen Square, Beijing, June 3–4, 1989, sparked worldwide outrage.

China's political future remains uncertain. China's leadership is aging—an ailing Deng is 91. His designated successor is President Jiang Zemin, 69, but others are jockeying for power, and a possibly destabilizing succession struggle may follow Deng's death.

China has been a nuclear power since 1964 and is building a modern military force. Its defense budget reportedly has grown by 10% a year since 1989, causing concern to the U.S. and its Asian neighbors. China is also a major exporter of arms.

Taiwan

The island of Taiwan, roughly half the size of Indiana, was occupied by Japan from 1895–1945. Taiwan reverted to Chinese rule after Japan's defeat in World War II. In the ensuing civil war in China, Mao's Communists drove Chiang Kai-shek and his Nationalist (Kuomintang) forces from the mainland to Taiwan. There Chiang established the Republic of China (ROC) and declared it the sole legitimate government of China.

China regards Taiwan as a "renegade province," and although it has a long-standing commitment to peaceful reunification with Taiwan, it does not rule out the use of military force.

In 1987, Chiang Ching-kuo, who had succeeded his father as ROC president in 1978, allowed informal relations with China to develop. Under his successor, Lee Teng-hui, the first native Taiwanese head of state, informal economic contacts with the mainland grew. At the same time Taiwan made great strides toward de-

Bob Mansfield

mocracy, culminating in the March 23, 1996, election, the first in the history of China in which a president had been directly elected. Lee won by a landslide.

Taiwan has the fourth-largest economy in East Asia and is the world's 12th-biggest trader. It boasts the world's second-largest foreign-exchange reserves—over $90 billion as of March 1996. Taiwan is also one of China's largest investors, with $30 billion worth of holdings in 1995. While it has extensive trade relations, Taiwan is recognized by none of the major powers. President Lee has spearheaded Taiwan's attempts for greater international recognition, including admission to the United Nations. In June 1995, Taiwan offered the cash-strapped world organization $1 billion if it agreed to accept it as a member, an offer the UN declined.

Beijing has used military intimidation to remind Taiwan that it is not a sovereign state but part of China. In March 1996, as Taiwan's voters prepared to go to the polls, China conducted a week of missile tests near two of Taiwan's leading seaports, Keelung and Kaohsiung. The following week China held military exercises in the Taiwan Strait. Chinese officials acknowledged these were acts of military intimidation intended to change Lee's behavior and deter the movement toward independence, which is favored by many of the native Taiwanese.

Hong Kong

Hong Kong became a British colony in the 19th century but will revert to Chinese rule on July 1, 1997, when Britain's 99-year lease on the territory expires. After the reversion, China plans to maintain Hong Kong as a Special Administrative Region for 50 years under a "one country, two systems" plan. Under the terms of a Sino-British agreement in 1984, Hong Kong's government will be autonomous except in defense and foreign affairs, and it will retain its capitalist economy, which has supplied China with over 60% of its foreign investment. Whether such a policy can work—a democracy and market economy surviving under a Communist central government—remains to be seen.

U.S.-China Relations

Until 1971, the ROC represented China in the UN. That year it was replaced by the PRC. In 1972, President Richard M. Nixon made a historic trip to Beijing. In 1978–79, the U.S. terminated its mutual defense treaty and severed formal relations with Taiwan, and it recognized the PRC. The Taiwan Relations Act of 1979, however, provides for continued informal contacts and notes that the U.S. will consider "any effort to determine the future of Taiwan by other than peaceful means...a threat to the peace and security of the Western Pacific area and of grave concern to the U.S." The U.S. conducts unofficial relations with Taiwan as a de facto separate entity.

The Clinton Administration favors a policy of "constructive engagement" with China. It considers a policy of dealing with China on various issues, including trade, security and human rights, preferable to confronting or isolating the Chinese leadership. "If we treat China as an enemy, it will almost certainly become one," notes Rep. Lee Hamilton (D-Ind.), ranking minority member of the House International Relations Committee.

Trade

U.S. trade with China has grown rapidly since 1979. In January 1980, Congress approved **most-favored-nation (MFN) status** for China, and a major bilateral trade pact was signed later that year. (MFN status is subject to annual review.) In 1980, Sino-American trade was valued at $4.8 billion. By 1995, it had grown by almost 1,300%.

During the 1992 presidential election campaign, candidate Bill Clinton denounced China's human-rights violations and favored tying MFN to an improvement in that area. In May 1994, however, President Clinton announced that he would renew China's MFN status irrespective of its human-rights record. Six months before the 1996 presidential election, Clinton again called for unconditional renewal of MFN trade status for China. Republican presidential candidate and former Senate Majority Leader Bob Dole, splitting with the conservative wing of his party, supported the decision, "not because it is in our economic interest but because it is in our national interest...."

Supporters of MFN renewal believe that economic progress will eventually lead to political liberalization and that keeping open the lines of communication to Beijing can aid the development of political freedom. Furthermore, supporters state that tying human rights

By Auth for the Philadelphia Inquirer. Reprinted with permission of Universal Press Syndicate. All rights reserved.

to trade privileges simply does not work. It hurts U.S. trade and cuts access to China's market while doing little to improve conditions in China. An estimated 200,000 American jobs are directly tied to U.S.-China trade.

Critics charge that American policy toward China is one of appeasement that places business interests over human-rights concerns. They note that only when the U.S. has applied pressure has China responded by freeing dissidents or opening its jails to inspection. China's MFN status was renewed by Congress in June 1996.

Another key irritant in the troubled U.S.-Sino relationship is China's violations of **intellectual property rights,** including copyrights and trademarks. Although the U.S. and China signed a copyright agreement in February 1995, enforcement of the accord has proved elusive. Chinese authorities crack down on plants producing pirated goods, only to have them spring up again. The situation is difficult because several manufacturers reportedly have ties to government officials and the People's Liberation Army. U.S. industries have estimated that piracy has cost them $2.2 billion in lost revenue. In February 1996, then U.S. Trade Representative Mickey Kantor called for sanctions, arguing that American credibility would suffer if Beijing was allowed to violate agreements with impunity. Three months later, the Clinton Administration published a list of $3 billion worth of Chinese goods that would be subject to 100% tariffs if Beijing did not shut down factories that pirated American goods by June 17, 1996. China retaliated by threatening to block new American investments and to place enormous tariffs on American automobiles, telecommunications equipment and other goods.

A trade war was averted when round-the-clock negotiations resulted in a broad agreement on June 17. China closed down two more pirate compact-disk factories and agreed to take steps to ban the reproduction and sale of pirated intellectual property. Threatened sanctions were averted.

Still another source of tension in U.S. relations with China is the burgeoning **U.S. trade deficit.** The deficit soared from $2 billion in the late 1980s to $34 billion in 1995. By opening its markets wider, China can improve trade relations with the U.S. as well as its chances of admission to the World Trade Organization (WTO), which sets and enforces the rules for global trade. Membership in the WTO would offer China major trade advantages, including the possibility of boosting its exports by as much as one third. The U.S. has stated it will not support China's application until it lowers import barriers, loosens controls on foreign investment and trade, and abides by international conventions, including those governing copyrights and patents.

Human rights

In March 1996, the U.S. annual human-rights report declared China guilty of "widespread and well-documented human-rights abuses," including torture, arbitrary detention, coercive family-planning practices and organ transplants drawn from executed prisoners. The report declared further that by the end of 1995 almost all public dissent against the central authorities had been silenced. After releasing the report, the U.S. announced it would again cosponsor a resolution critical of China at the UN Human Rights Commission session in Geneva, Switzerland. Beijing, however, used a procedural rule to bar the introduction of even a mildly critical resolution at the session, dealing a major blow to the Clinton Administration and the authority of the commission.

Taiwan

U.S. contacts with Taiwan have become a major irritant in U.S.-China relations. When the U.S. decided to issue President Lee a visa for a "private" visit in 1995, relations between Washington and Beijing soured. China recalled its ambassador to the U.S. in June 1995 (he returned in August); delayed approval of former Sen. James Sasser of Tennessee as U.S. ambassador to China; suspended bilateral talks on nonproliferation and human rights; and rounded up dozens of dissidents on the eve of the sixth anniversary of the Tiananmen Square massacre.

The U.S. responded to China's intimidation of Taiwan in March 1996 with a show of force unprecedented since the Vietnam War. The White House dispatched two aircraft-carrier groups to monitor the situation. The

U.S. did not state whether it would defend Taiwan if war erupted, and it continues to urge the peaceful settlement of the China-Taiwan question by the two parties.

Conciliatory gestures from both sides of the strait helped defuse the crisis soon after the March election, and the American naval carriers returned to their posts.

Arms exports

In 1995 the U.S. learned that China, a major arms exporter, had delivered more than 30 medium-range ballistic missiles to Pakistan and supplied Iran with unspecified missile technologies. In February 1996 China allegedly transferred to Pakistan 5,000 specialized magnets used to enrich uranium for nuclear arms. China and Pakistan denied the reports. Such exports violate the Nuclear Nonproliferation Treaty (NPT) of 1968, are banned under the Missile Technology Control Regime and may violate U.S. law. China is a 1992 signatory to the NPT.

Sen. Arlen Specter (R-Penn.), chair of the Senate Intelligence Committee, called on President Clinton "to impose the maximum sanctions available" under U.S. law for the nuclear-related sales. The Administration considered but in the end rejected harsh sanctions that would have banned economic and military aid, cut off international loans and eliminated $10 billion in loan guarantees to American companies, hurting U.S. workers and companies like Boeing and Westinghouse, along with the Chinese. In return, Beijing promised not to transfer nuclear-related items in the future, reconfirmed its commitment to stopping the spread of nuclear weapons, and agreed to consult with Washington on export-control policies and other proliferation issues. Critics of Clinton's decision complained that he had made national-security interests subservient to U.S. corporate interests. Given China's record of arms exports, Rep. Nancy Pelosi (D-Calif.) believes "the Administration seems to have settled yet again for an empty promise."

China conducted an underground nuclear test as recently as June 8, 1996, and plans one final test by September. On June 6, China announced it had abandoned its long-standing insistence on its right to conduct "peaceful" nuclear tests and was prepared to sign a comprehensive test-ban treaty that is being drafted for signature before the end of the year. However, China objects to what it considers overly intrusive verification methods for compliance with the ban.

Hong Kong

In 1992, Congress passed the U.S.-Hong Kong Policy Act under which the U.S., after the Chinese takeover in 1997, will continue to treat Hong Kong as a separate entity in those areas in which it retains autonomy.

Policy Choices

1. **The U.S. should continue the present policy of "constructive engagement."**

- ❑ **Yes:** China is the fastest-growing economy in the world and a formidable regional and world power. The two countries have much to offer each other, including trade and investment opportunities, technology sharing, and military and defense cooperation.

- ❑ **No:** China is bent on playing a larger, more aggressive role in the Asia-Pacific and must be deterred and contained, not engaged. In addition to violating trade rules, it has exported missiles to regional hot spots, violated agreements to prevent the spread of nuclear technology, and threatened the security of Northeast Asia by sending missiles into the Taiwan Strait.

2. **The U.S. should continue to grant MFN status to China.**

- ❑ **Yes:** Denying China MFN would not hurt China; it would benefit our competitors. Threats to stop trade or apply sanctions only undermine the chances for good long-term commercial ties, which remain the best hope for peaceful coexistence.

- ❑ **No:** China has flouted bilateral and international agreements. The U.S. should impose sanctions, either across-the-board or selected ones that do the least harm to U.S. business. America's failure to punish China hurts U.S. credibility.

3. **The U.S. should assist China's entry to the World Trade Organization.**
- ❏ **Yes:** It is preferable to have China in the club where it can be held accountable.
- ❏ **No:** China must first demonstrate a willingness to abide by international norms.

4. **The U.S. should take a trade-policy stand against China's human-rights violations.**
- ❏ **Yes:** It is immoral to do business with a country that violates human rights. The U.S. must penalize China, even if it hurts U.S. companies, to prove that Americans hate tyranny more than they love trade, to paraphrase conservative Republican presidential candidate Patrick J. Buchanan.
- ❏ **No:** Internal economic change remains the best hope for creating conditions for a more liberal China. The U.S. should continue to denounce China's human-rights violations in the UN and in bilateral talks, but not mix rights with trade.

5. **The U.S. should recognize and defend Taiwan.**
- ❏ **Yes:** The U.S. has more in common with democratic Taiwan than it does with authoritarian China, and it should recognize Taiwan as an independent state. The U.S. should be prepared to use force if necessary to defend it.
- ❏ **No:** U.S. renunciation of the "one China" policy could lead to war. An unconditional promise to defend Taiwan could encourage the Taiwanese to provoke an attack or could prompt China to start a war with Taiwan. The U.S. should not recognize Taiwan and thus avoid a confrontation with another nuclear power.

Select Bibliography

"China." *Current History*, Sept. 1995. Entire issue devoted to China, Greater China and U.S.-Chinese relations.

Ching, Frank, "Hong Kong and China: 'One Country, Two Systems'?" *Headline Series* No. 310. New York, Foreign Policy Association, 1996. Examines the implications of Hong Kong's reversion to Chinese sovereignty for the British colony's people, economy and its trading partners, as well as the future of U.S.-Chinese relations.

Goldstein, Steven M., "China at the Crossroads: Reform After Tiananmen." *Headline Series* No. 298 (double issue). New York, Foreign Policy Association, 1992. Analyzes the major trends in China since the Tiananmen crisis in 1989 and discusses the implications of these trends for U.S. policy.

Lord, Winston, "The United States and the Security of Taiwan." *U.S. Department of State Dispatch*, Feb. 5, 1996, pp. 29–32. Assistant secretary for East Asian and Pacific affairs outlines current U.S. policy toward Taiwan.

———, "U.S. Policy Toward China: Security and Military Considerations." *U.S. Department of State Dispatch*, Oct. 23, 1995, pp. 773–75. Assistant secretary explains the Clinton Administration's policy toward China.

Overholt, William H., "China after Deng." *Foreign Affairs*, May/June 1996, pp. 63–78. Managing director in charge of Asian research for Bankers Trust believes China "is headed in the right direction."

4

Russia

✔ *Where is Russia headed in this period of transition from Communist rule?*

✔ *Are increasing nationalism and the Communist resurgence in Russia cause for U.S. concern?*

✔ *How should the U.S. respond to Russian militarism in breakaway republics like Chechnya and in the 'near abroad'?*

✔ *Is U.S. aid helping Russia's transition to democracy and capitalism?*

✔ *How can the U.S. expedite the reduction of Russia's nuclear stockpile?*

Basic Facts

- **Population:** 149.9 million (1995)
- **Area:** 6.6 million sq. mi. covering 11 time zones, from Urals to the Pacific
- **Government:** Federation of 89 republics, oblasts and krais
- **President:** Boris N. Yeltsin, elected June 12, 1991; Yeltsin and Gennadi A. Zyuganov, finalists in presidential runoff election in July 1996.
- **Prime Minister:** Viktor S. Chernomyrdin

- Parliament: In the December 1995 elections, the Communist party reclaimed a majority (22.3%) of seats in the State Duma (lower house of parliament).
- **Independence from Soviet Union** declared December 8, 1991.
- Ratified **Start I treaty** with the U.S., and is working toward the specified limit of 6,000 strategic warheads.
- Ratification of **Start II,** limiting strategic warheads to 3,500, is pending.
- Spent **$63 billion on defense** in 1995 (down from $110 billion in 1990 for the Soviet Union), the second highest military budget in the world.
- Joined NATO's Partnership for Peace Program in June 1994.

Background

Russia is at a critical point in its history as it makes the transition from more than 70 years of communism to democracy and capitalism. A successful conversion to a multiparty democratic state with a market economy will probably lead to cooperation between the U.S. and Russia. However, the failure of reform, possibly resulting from a return to power of antireform Communists, could lead to renewed confrontation with the West.

Russia faces the task of establishing a capitalist economy in a country with no capitalist traditions or institutions. The Communist system eliminated industrial competition, established huge collective farms and factories, and forbade private ownership of the means of production. All economic activity was dictated by a central planning committee, rather than by managers of individual factories or farms. Freedom of speech, press and religion was restricted and political opposition groups were forbidden.

In the mid-1980s, Soviet President Mikhail S. Gorbachev instituted programs to allow some individual economic freedoms and constructive criticism of the Communist system. Gorbachev also developed a close

42 ■ Russia

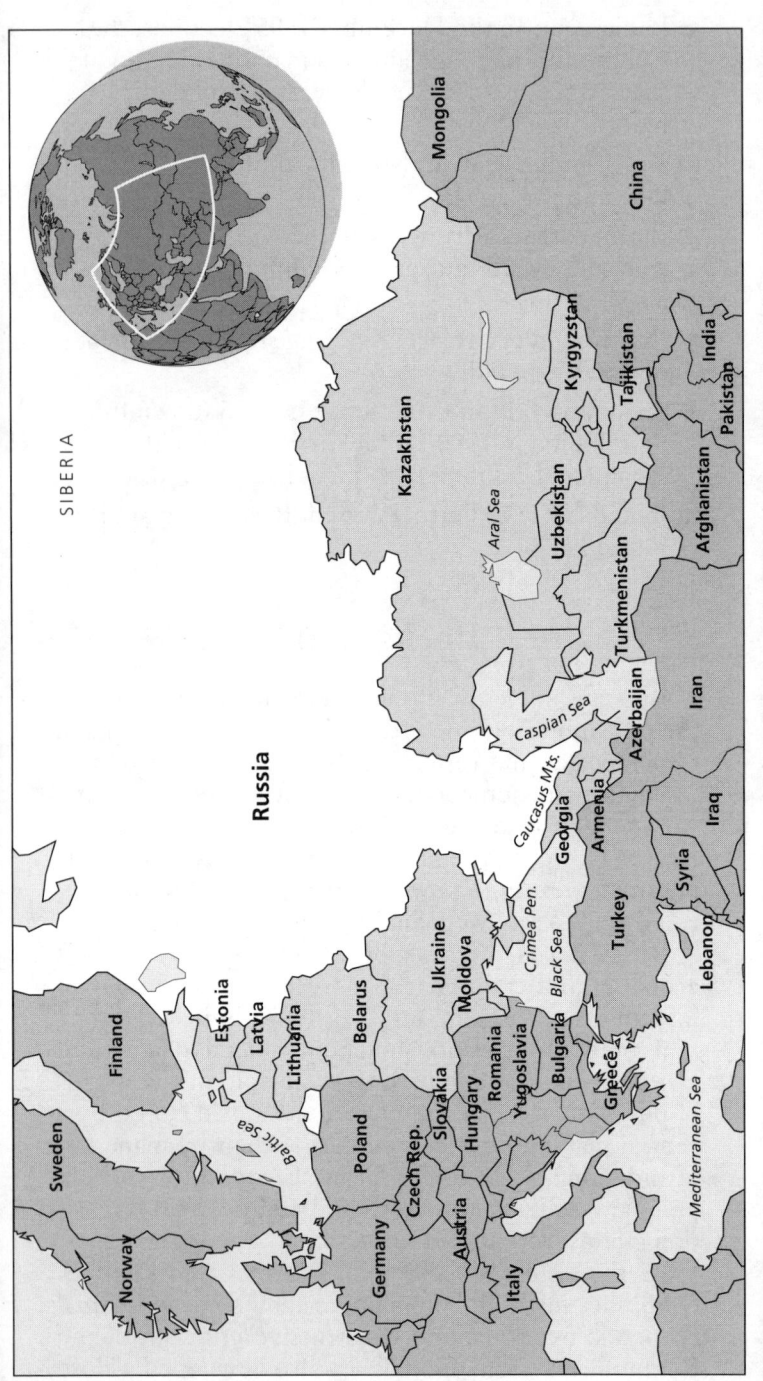

Bob Mansfield

relationship with Western leaders. These two policies contributed to the dissolution of the Soviet Union in 1991 and the rise of Boris Yeltsin. Yeltsin became the driving force behind the economic and political reform process which continues today.

Economic reform

Yeltsin implemented numerous measures to allow greater political participation and introduce a market economy. Some worked; others are still being carried out. The Soviet economy had been geared toward the production of military goods and basic foodstuffs. When Yeltsin cut defense spending and left the conversion of military factories to new owners, Russia suffered from the lack of a diversified economy. Despite selling off numerous state-owned industries to private investors, the Russian government continues to own many factories, leading to continued inefficiency in production and reliance upon outdated technologies. High unemployment and hyperinflation have wiped out the savings of retired workers. Nostalgia for the "good old days" among older Russians fueled the recent resurgence of nationalists and Communists led by Gennadi Zyuganov.

By selling off much of the Soviet industrial base to private citizens, Russia has taken the first steps toward institutionalizing a market economy. Land reform is also under way, but it has progressed less quickly than industrial reform. Some observers see the economic reform process as flawed. They note that the privatization of industry favored individuals who could quickly amass a large sum of money. Typically, these were the managers of factories, many of whom obtained their money in a questionable, if not illegal, manner. Land reform is proceeding slowly amid controversy over how the huge collective farms may best be broken up. The lack of a stable banking system and laws to protect small businesses have led to the rise of organized crime, threatening the nascent private sector in Russia.

The Clinton Administration is committed to the process of reform in Russia and to Yeltsin. Despite high inflation, shortages of goods, higher crime and unemployment, the U.S. believes Russia is making good progress toward institutionalizing capitalism. Economic reforms are expected to provide a higher standard of living, reversing the current trend of declining life expectancy, resurgence of preventable diseases, and increasing poverty. To demonstrate his support of Yeltsin's reelection, President Bill Clinton attended a meeting in April 1996 to showcase Yeltsin as a world leader. In fall 1995, Clinton lobbied the International Monetary Fund (IMF) to grant Russia an additional loan of $10.2 billion. Since 1992, Russia has received $9.8 billion from the IMF and $6.4 billion from the World Bank.

In addition to the IMF and World Bank loans, Russia has received some $3 billion from the U.S. In 1992, Congress approved the Freedom Support Act to help Russia convert to a market-oriented, privately owned economy, to introduce and reinforce democratic principles and processes, and to promote services and programs to improve the quality of life. For fiscal year 1996, Congress approved $147.7 million for the Freedom Support Act, substantially less than the $260 million requested by the Administration. President Clinton supports further aid to Russia in order to secure the reforms already implemented and to help Russia continue its transition to democracy and a market economy. Republican presidential candidate and former Senate Majority Leader Bob Dole feels that Russia has forgotten or ignored U.S. interests and that Washington should give aid only as long as Russia pursues policies in harmony with American interests.

Political reform

Russia has made significant progress in forming a more open and democratic government. Although the constitution adopted by referendum in December 1993 grants the executive overwhelming power, it also assigns substantive powers to the legislature. In addition, Russian citizens enjoy such freedoms as the right to free speech. This has led to the emergence of a great number of independent newspapers and television stations, as well as opposition political parties.

Will Russia maintain the momentum toward democracy? Observers point to incidents of journalists being murdered as evidence that the press does not enjoy complete freedom in Russia. There is even the fear that

Yeltsin himself is less committed to reform than he once was. In response to the rising challenge from the nationalists and Communists, Yeltsin increasingly embraced authoritarian symbols, policies and advisers in his presidential campaign. However, after winning the first round of the elections, he purged some of the most hard-line, antidemocratic and antireform aides.

Republicans charge Clinton with placing too much emphasis on supporting the reformer rather than the reform process. Yeltsin had been hailed as a Russian savior for helping to end the August 1991 coup by hardliners that ousted Gorbachev and for accelerating the Soviet Union's demise. But his dissolution of the democratically elected parliament in 1993 and the seige of the parliament building by the army raised questions about Yeltsin's commitment to democracy. Since that time, his critics charge, Yeltsin has shown two faces to the world: that of a pro-Western democrat, usually worn for the benefit of the U.S. and others who have vowed to help Russia through its economic difficulties, and that of an autocrat, used to bringing dissenting and opposing states, peoples and parties into line. The U.S. has often been frustrated in its attempts to cultivate Yeltsin as a leader of a free and open society. For this reason, Republicans question the Clinton Administration's belief in the importance of Yeltsin to U.S.-Russian relations.

Military affairs

The U.S. and others have also been concerned about Yeltsin's handling of the crisis in Chechnya in the Caucasus. The Chechens, a people with a historic desire for independence, declared Chechen-Ingushetia's secession from the Soviet Union on November 1, 1991. On November 30, Ingushetia voted to remain part of the Russian Federation; however, Chechens refused even to participate in the elections, insisting upon complete independence and thus severing themselves from Ingushetians as well as the Russian Federation. In December 1994, Yeltsin ordered a full-scale invasion of Chechnya. The conflict mushroomed into a drawn-out, bloody campaign which has claimed the lives not only of soldiers but thousands of civilians. Stories of Russian

Toles©The Buffalo News. Reprinted with permission of Universal Press Syndicate. All rights reserved.

brutality in Chechnya have caused outrage toward Russia. The Russian military has also been embarrassed by its failure to quell the rebellion. Although a cease-fire agreement was signed in Moscow on May 27, 1996, the rebellion is far from over.

Some critics fault the Clinton Administration for not speaking out against Russia's actions in Chechnya. Supporters defend the Administration's handling of the situation, suggesting that the Chechen situation, like the American Civil War, is a domestic matter that should be left to the Russians to handle.

Some policymakers are concerned that the Chechen crisis could precipitate the splintering of Russia and its loss of control over its nuclear weapons. Russia and the U.S., which possess nuclear arsenals capable of destroying each other, have reached a series of agreements to help alleviate the threat. Yeltsin and Clinton agreed in January 1994 to stop targeting their strategic nuclear missiles at each other as of May 30, 1994. In 1993, both Russia and the U.S. signed the Treaty on Further Reduction and Limitation of Strategic Offensive Arms (Start II). Under this treaty, each country will reduce its arsenal of strategic nuclear weapons by more than two thirds and will eliminate the most destabilizing of these weapons—heavy intercontinental ballistic missiles (ICBMs) and all other missiles with multiple warheads. Instead of waiting the prescribed nine years once the treaty is ratified, each side agreed, at a September 1994 summit, to begin immediately dismantling the missiles outlawed under Start II.

Critics point out that despite these positive steps there is still cause for concern. In recent months, powerful members of the Russian parliament have denounced the Start II treaty, claiming it guts the heart of the Russian nuclear arsenal (land-based ICBMs) and leaves the U.S. with the core of its force (bombers and submarine-launched ballistic missiles) intact. Russia has also objected to what it sees as the potential U.S. violation of the 1972 Anti-Ballistic Missile (ABM) Treaty as a result of the development of a missile defense system. Some Russian legislators insist on linking U.S. compliance with the ABM Treaty to ratification of Start II. Critics also question whether Russia has full control over its nuclear weapons and nuclear materials. They note that facilities housing the vast quantities of weapons-grade materials produced during the cold war are poorly guarded. In recent years, there have been frequent incidents of stolen nuclear materials, such as the seizure of some six pounds of enriched uranium by Czech officials in 1994.

Clinton strongly supported ratification and implementation of Start II, despite the delay in the Russian parliament; and he continues to support the ABM Treaty. The best way to combat the poor security of nuclear facilities in Russia and to facilitate the dismantlement of the Russian nuclear arsenal, the Clinton Administration maintains, is through continued aid to Russia. Under the "Cooperative Threat Reduction" program, also called Nunn-Lugar assistance, the U.S. has provided $1.5 billion to the countries of the former Soviet Union, including over $750 million to Russia alone, to increase security and help dismantle and store nuclear weapons.

Dole supports Nunn-Lugar aid to Russia, but he advocates greater selectivity in allocating funds. Dole believes economic aid to Russia and the other former republics should be based on their record of support for U.S. interests. To receive U.S. aid, he would expect Russia to back Western policy and enforce strictly the nonproliferation of weapons of mass destruction and nuclear technology.

Dole believes the U.S. should set aside the ABM Treaty, regardless of Russian opposition, in order to develop further U.S. ballistic-missile-defense technology. Dole defines the issue as a security issue rather than a question of relations with Russia. The U.S. must be able to defend itself against a ballistic-missile attack. Critics charge such a policy could begin a new arms race.

Foreign relations

The Chechen war has raised U.S. fears that Russia may try to assert control over former Soviet territory. Most of the 14 other states that made up the U.S.S.R. contain large minority populations of ethnic Russians and Russian army troops. Since the Soviet breakup, Russia has been involved in numerous altercations with its "near abroad" neighbors. The contentious issue of the Black Sea Fleet between Russia and Ukraine was resolved by splitting the fleet. Although Russian troops stationed in the near abroad are almost all under the command of local authorities, in several cases Russian troops have taken sides in factional fighting, particularly in Georgia, Tajikistan and Azerbaijan. Some analysts point to two recent treaties establishing economic and political ties between Russia and its neighbors as further evidence that Russia wants to rebuild the Soviet empire. One of these, the April 1996 agreement between Russia and Belarus, all but reunites the two countries. The other treaty, signed by Russia, Belarus, Kyrgyzstan and Kazakhstan in March 1996, calls for the free movement of goods, services, labor and capital between the states. Russia, for its part, is opposed to expansion of NATO into Eastern Europe and the Baltics. Russia views this expansion, and the potential basing of nuclear weapons there, as a threat to its security.

Of further concern to the U.S. is Russia's handling of relations with countries outside the borders of the former U.S.S.R. Russia's claim to the Kuril Islands, taken from

Japan at the end of World War II, was at the heart of diplomatic sparring in 1993 and 1994 between the two states. In 1995, Russia agreed to help Iran construct a nuclear reactor. The U.S. is concerned that the reactor will produce weapons-grade nuclear materials, possibly enabling Iran to acquire nuclear weapons. Some see a threat in the recent security pact between Russia and China, particularly in light of Beijing's recent military intimidation of Taiwan. They fear that Russia's expansion of ties with the near abroad and with states hostile to the U.S. could lead to the return of a cold-war mentality in Moscow.

Russian Communists and some nationalists have called for the peaceful reintegration of all "lost" Soviet territory. (Nationalist Vladimir Zhirinovsky even suggests reclaiming Alaska which Russia sold to the U.S. in 1867.)

Administration Policy

Both Clinton and Dole support continued Russian reform. They differ, however, in the way they believe the U.S. can help the reform process and the way in which the U.S. should respond to Russia's domestic policies and relationships with its near abroad.

Clinton is willing to provide substantial aid to Russia in the expectation that Russia will continue to implement democratic and economic reforms. Privately, the Clinton Administration believes Yeltsin is the best candidate to carry out the reforms. However, the Administration has expressed its belief in the democratic system and stated that if the Communists won the presidential election, the U.S. would work with them. Clinton hopes to avoid alienating Russia and igniting nationalist, anti-Western sympathies and at the same time strengthen ties between the two countries.

Dole and the Republican party agree that democratic and market reforms are the key to good relations with Russia in the future, but subscribe to a harder-line approach. Dole supports faster expansion of NATO into Eastern Europe and abrogation of the ABM Treaty. In addition, Republicans have been much more vocal about their opposition to the Communist party in Russia,

Yeltsin's failings, and their belief that all U.S. aid to Russia should be conditioned on how well the Russian government supports U.S. interests.

The difference in policy between the two candidates is less about goals than about the method of achieving them.

Policy Choices

1. **Aid:**
- ❏ a. The U.S. should continue to provide substantial aid to Russia in order to help spur economic growth, prod the reform process, ensure the security of Russia's nuclear arsenals and maintain a stable democratic leadership.

    OR

- ❏ b. The U.S. should withhold or restrict aid until Russia makes a stronger commitment to abide by arms treaties and human-rights accords to which it is a signatory and refrain from interfering in the former territories of the Soviet Union. U.S. aid to Russia should be a reward for progress made rather than an incentive for undertaking reforms.

2. **Military Affairs:**
- ❏ a. The U.S. should expand NATO regardless of Russian objections, press forward with a missile defense system even at the expense of violating the 1972 ABM Treaty and continue to pursue nuclear-weapons reductions.

    OR

- ❏ b. The U.S. should halt or postpone the expansion of NATO in deference to Russia's concerns and honor the ABM treaty to avoid precipitating a new arms race.

Select Bibliography

Heilbrunn, Jacob, "The Big East." *The New Republic*, May 27, 1996, pp. 22–24. The possibility of Russian threats to U.S. interests is discussed.

Lynch, Allen, "Russia and Its Neighbors: U.S. Policy

Choices." *Great Decisions 1995*, pp. 25–34. New York, Foreign Policy Association, 1995. Analyzes the historic significance of the Soviet Union's disintegration.

Matlock, Jack F., Jr., "Dealing with a Russia in Turmoil." *Foreign Affairs*, May/June 1996, pp. 38–51. Examines the current turmoil in Russian politics and U.S. policy toward Russia.

McFaul, Michael, "Russian Politics: The Calm Before the Storm?" *Current History*, Oct. 1994, pp. 313–19. Discusses the power struggle between Yeltsin and Russian parliament.

"U.S.-Russian Economic Relations and Military Issues." *U.S. Department of State Fact Sheet*, Feb. 1, 1996, pp. 1–3. Available free from the State Department Public Affairs Office. Tel.: (202) 647-6575. Outlines specific treaties and agreements between the U.S. and Russia since the cold war ended.

5

Mexico

✔ *Should the U.S. continue to support the North American Free Trade Agreement (Nafta)?*

✔ *Is Mexico doing enough to combat illegal drug trafficking?*

✔ *Should the U.S. tighten restrictions on illegal immigration from Mexico?*

Basic Facts

1995	Mexico	U.S.
Real GDP	$250 billion	$7.2 trillion
Per capita GDP	$2,741	$27,530
Real GDP growth rate	-6.9%	2%
Population	91.2 million	263.2 million
Unemployment	16.2%	5.6%

	1994	1995
Mexican exports to U.S.	$49.5 billion	$61.7 billion
Mexican imports from the U.S.	$50.8 billion	$46.3 billion
U.S. trade balance with Mexico	$1.3 billion	-$15.4 billion

Background

Extending southeastward from the 2,000-mile-long border with the U.S. to the jungles of Yucatán and Guatemala, Mexico is a federal republic with 31 states and a federal district of Mexico City. It won independence from Spain in 1810 and became a republic in 1822. Since World War II, Mexico has undergone rapid industrialization, but the benefits have been unequally shared. Almost one fourth of the population still lives off the land. Of the 75% who live in urban areas, many need jobs, housing and health care. Mexico is endowed with mineral and energy resources. Tourism is the country's third-largest industry. Its beaches and archaeological sites attract visitors from all over the world. It is the world's fifth-largest oil producer, and it is this country's third-largest trade partner.

Since 1929 one political party—the Institutional Revolutionary Party (PRI)—has dominated the elections and the bureaucracy. The president, currently Ernesto Zedillo Ponce de León, is directly elected for a six-year term. He is also the de facto head of the PRI, which gives him a monopoly over patronage. Presidents may not be reelected, but they have traditionally had a decisive voice in selecting their successors.

A founding member of the United Nations and the Organization of American States (OAS), Mexico generally follows an independent foreign policy based on the principles of nonintervention and self-determination.

Economic and political reforms

After a period of rapid economic growth (6% a year in 1970–75 and 8% in 1976–81), Mexico fell into a deep recession. Capital took flight and unemployment and inflation soared. In 1982, Mexico announced it was unable to pay its huge foreign debt. President Miguel de la Madrid Hurtado (1982–88) opened up Mexico's tightly regulated economy, resulting in a dramatic increase in the flow of trade and investment. This policy was continued by Carlos Salinas de Gortari (1988–94), an advocate of economic liberalization and market-oriented reforms. In the early 1990s, Salinas rekindled economic growth, reduced inflation, privatized hundreds of state firms and attracted billions of investment dollars. His successor, Ernesto Zedillo, who was inaugurated on December 1, 1994, had barely assumed office when the fiscal crisis of 1994–95 shattered the recovery and gave rise to serious new socioeconomic and political problems. President Zedillo pledged to strengthen the economic reforms, combat poverty, expand political pluralism and competition and overhaul the justice system. Multiparty agreements in December 1995 paved the way for ending the PRI's monopoly and reshaping authoritarian institutions.

Political instability

In early 1994, an uprising broke out in the southern state of Chiapas. The Zapatista National Liberation Army (EZLN), led by the university-trained Sub-commander Marcos and consisting of several hundred Indian guerrillas, issued the Declaration of the Lacandona Jungle in which they sought redress from a "dictatorship of more than 70 years." The rebellion was endorsed by Roman Catholic Bishop Samuel Ruiz Garcia, a liberation theologian who had long crusaded for the rights of Indian peasants. (Some politicians and conservative Catholic leaders accused Ruiz of helping to foment the insurrection in Chiapas.) The assassinations of presidential candidate Luis Donaldo Colosio

Murrieta in March 1994 and José Francisco Ruiz Massieu, a Salinas ally and the PRI's secretary-general, in September 1994, intensified the sense of crisis generated by the Chiapas insurgency. The assassinations remain unsolved.

Clashes between the Zapatistas and the government continued through 1995. On January 1, 1996, the Zapatistas announced plans to form a new political opposition movement that would be peaceful and nonmilitary. A little over a month later, representatives of the EZLN, the Mexican federal government and the state government of Chiapas signed the first of six formal peace accords giving Indians more political control and representation in the national congress. The remaining five accords were to address more controversial issues such as judicial reform and property rights.

1994–95 financial crisis

Mexico's economic growth rate declined from 3.6% in 1991 to less than 1% in 1993, but rebounded in 1994. At the same time, inflation fell from 15.5% in 1992 to 7.1% in 1994. An overvalued currency, combined with the diminishing inflationary gap between Mexico and its main trading partner, the U.S., made imports relatively cheap. This contributed to a growing current-account deficit, which reached $28 billion by December 1994. The eventual sharp devaluation of the peso by about a third against the dollar pushed the country into a deep economic crisis. The Mexican president announced an emergency program, including federal budget cuts and more privatization, but these measures failed to restore investor confidence in the short term. By the end of 1995, the gross domestic product (GDP) had declined 6.9%. The crisis increased unemployment and severely hurt Mexico's business community, middle class and blue-collar workers.

U.S.-Mexican Relations

Mexico lost one half of its territory to the U.S. in the mid-19th century and remains sensitive about U.S. intervention in its affairs. Relations between the two countries have generally been cordial since World War II, although there was some tension in the late 1970s when Mexico backed Third World demands for a greater voice in the international economic system and supported the left-wing Sandinista government in Nicaragua. The major issues that divide the U.S. and Mexico in the 1990s are trade, drug trafficking and immigration. These are addressed in annual summit meetings of high-level U.S. and Mexican officials.

Trade

In 1988–89, the U.S. pledged to support Mexico's economic reform efforts and negotiate a debt-reduction agreement. In 1990, Mexico dropped its opposition to trade talks with the U.S. and formally requested the opening of negotiations. Discussions commenced in mid-1991 and concluded with the signing of the North American Free Trade Agreement (Nafta) between the U.S., Mexico and Canada. Nafta's entry into force on January 1, 1994, resulted in the immediate elimination of duties on about one half of U.S. exports to Mexico and the beginning of progressive reductions in the remaining tariffs over a 15-year period. Nafta was supplemented by agreements on the environment, labor and import surges. In 1994, the first year of Nafta, bilateral exchange of goods and services exceeded $100 billion, up 17.5% from 1993. In 1995, however, the U.S. ran a trade deficit with Mexico of over $15 billion. Many members of U.S. organized labor claim that Nafta is costing the country factories and jobs. Others attribute the trade deficit primarily to Mexico's peso devaluation and subsequent rising demand for Mexican exports in America, and they maintain it is unrelated to Nafta. Mexican critics of Nafta in turn blame the pact for Mexico's crisis and consider it a license for the U.S. to intrude in their country's internal affairs.

Drug trafficking

With its large land mass, sparsely populated areas and extensive frontier with the U.S., Mexico is a convenient base for drug trafficking and drug-money laundering. As much as 70% of the cocaine produced by Colombian drug cartels that enters the U.S. is smuggled in by Mexican crime organizations. The U.S. has criticized Mexico for not being more aggressive in combating the narcotics trade. To counter U.S. criticism, Mexican authorities in January 1996 arrested and expelled to the U.S. Juan Garcia Abrego, a billionaire drug trafficker who was on the FBI's 10 Most Wanted list. (In another concession to the U.S., Mexico reversed its long-standing opposition to extradition and in April for the first time extradited two men wanted by the U.S.). While critics still regard Mexico's performance as unsatisfactory, the Administration certified on March 1, 1996, that Mexico was cooperating with international efforts to stop narcotics trafficking. The decision to "decertify" Mexico would have disqualified it from receiving most U.S. economic aid.

In April 1996 Mexico reached an agreement with the U.S. providing for the transfer of 20 U.S. helicopters to the Mexican Air Force and the training of Mexican soldiers in antinarcotics tactics at Fort Bragg, North Carolina.

Illegal immigration

Mexican illegal immigration to the U.S. shows no signs of abating. Some 300,000 illegal aliens enter and remain in the U.S. each year. Of these, close to half crossed the Mexican border to get to the U.S. The numbers actually apprehended at the border are much higher, because many who fail the first time try a second and third crossing. Mexican officials, who have traditionally defended the rights of migrant workers, were outraged last April by the videotaped beating of two Mexican undocumented workers by Riverside County, California, sheriff's deputies. Mexican authorities called the beatings a "flagrant violation of human rights of Mexican citizens." On its own border with Guatemala and Belize, however, Mexico is known to disregard the human rights of illegal immigrants from Central America.

Mexico and the U.S. in April agreed on a pilot program, financed by Washington, in which illegal immigrants caught at the border can choose to be flown back home to central Mexico. In May the U.S. promised to advise Mexican diplomats whenever pregnant Mexican women or children were detained.

Legislation pending in Congress in mid-1996 would double the Border Patrol. In the meantime, the U.S. Immigration and Naturalization Service (INS) has toughened penalties, including prosecution and prison, for illegal entry into the U.S.

Many U.S. employers benefit from low-wage migrant workers, while others resent illegal immigration. In November 1994, 59% of California's voters approved Proposition 187, which denies education, health and social services to illegal immigrants and requires service providers to identify all persons suspected of being illegal immigrants. Because its constitutionality has been challenged, the proposition has not been enforced.

Administration Policy

The Administration supported Salinas's economic austerity program and has backed Zedillo's efforts to stabilize the economy and initiate political reforms.

In Mexico's 1994–95 fiscal crisis, President Bill Clinton, fearing widespread repercussions in other emerging market economies, promptly moved to mobilize $40 billion in credits for Mexico. When Congress balked at approving this rescue operation, President Clinton worked with the U.S. Treasury, the International Monetary Fund and other governments to create a $52 billion international aid packet, of which the U.S. provided $20 billion. Mexico repaid the U.S. Treasury $700

By Oliphant. Reprinted with permission of Universal Press Syndicate. All rights reserved.

million in late 1995, $1.3 billion in January 1996, and in June 1996 announced that it was repaying $4.7 billion. U.S. officials hailed the latest announcement as evidence that the Mexican economy is recovering.

The Administration continues to support Nafta but with some reservations. For example, in December 1995 the U.S. backed away from implementing the Nafta provision permitting Mexican trucks to move without restrictions in the U.S. The U.S. wants Mexico to impose tougher standards for training and licensing of drivers, improve safety standards and increase enforcement of drug laws.

Free trade is a major issue in the U.S. 1996 presidential campaign. The cheaper peso and diminished demand for U.S. goods in Mexico in 1995 resulted in a current-account surplus for Mexico. This encouraged two early Republican presidential candidates, TV commentator Patrick J. Buchanan and U.S. businessman Morry Taylor, and other free-trade critics to call for U.S. withdrawal from Nafta. Three other candidates, former Senate Majority Leader Bob Dole, former Tennessee governor Lamar Alexander and publisher Steve Forbes, supported free trade and Nafta.

On January 6, 1996, President Clinton signed legislation increasing the INS budget to $2.6 billion from the $2.1 billion provided in 1995. In his State of the Union Message to Congress on January 23, 1996, President Clinton reaffirmed his support for stiffened border protection and announced that he would "sign an executive order to deny federal contracts to businesses that hire illegal immigrants."

Policy Options

1. The U.S. should withdraw from Nafta.

❑ **Yes.** (1) Nafta has not benefited the U.S. economy: the U.S. imported more from Mexico in 1995 than it exported for the first time since 1990, at a cost of some 60,000 U.S. jobs. (2) Low-wage Mexican labor creates unfair competition for U.S. workers. (3) Eliminating trade barriers contributes to unfettered drug and human traffic across the border.

❑ **No.** (1) The U.S. trade deficit is unrelated to Nafta. Mexico's severe economic problems in 1995 made American goods too expensive for Mexican consumers. (2) Greater exports to Mexico in the long run will create more and better jobs in the U.S. In 1994 alone Nafta supported 130,000 export-related jobs in the U.S. (3) It is strategically important for the U.S. to have a stable, friendly and prosperous neighbor in Mexico. Nafta benefits both economies.

2. The U.S. should pressure Mexico to step up its war on drugs.

❑ **Yes.** (1) The flow of drugs from Mexico has not abated. (2) Corruption within Mexico's law-enforcement apparatus and the unwillingness of many officials to deal with the drug mafia contribute to easy drug smuggling.

❑ **No.** (1) The U.S. should avoid offending Mexican national sensibilities by an overly aggressive posture on drugs. More Mexican law-enforcement personnel (150) have died in border drug warfare than have their U.S. counterparts. (2) The key to combating the drug traffic is to eradicate the strong demand for drugs in the U.S.

3. The U.S. should do more to curb illegal immigration.

❑ **Yes.** (1) For more than a generation, public opinion polls have indicated overwhelming support among Americans for policies that discourage illegal immigration. In a democracy, policymakers are compelled to respond to their constituents' wishes. (2) Illegal immigrants are a burden on taxpayers and take jobs away from Americans.

❑ **No.** (1) Restrictive policies such as denying education and health services to illegal immigrants and their families violate basic human rights. (2) Migrant workers perform some jobs that would not be performed by unemployed U.S.-born workers. Mexican workers come to the U.S. because there is demand for their labor.

Select Bibliography

Grayson, George, "Mexico: Embattled Neighbor." *Great Decisions 1996*, pp. 23–32. New York, Foreign Policy Association, 1996. Overview of the current economic and political situation in Mexico and U.S.-Mexican relations.

———, *The North American Free Trade Agreement: Regional Community and the New World Order.* Lanham, Md., University Press of America, 1995.

Kryzanek, Michael, *U.S.-Latin American Relations.* Westport, Conn., Greenwood, 1996. Key issues in U.S.-Mexican relations.

"NAFTA." *The Year in Trade.* Washington, D.C., U.S. International Trade Commission Publication 2894, 1995, pp. 41–52. Report on the operation of Nafta.

"Reshaping America: Blurring Boundaries Between Mexico and the U.S." Report of the Thirty-Sixth Strategy for Peace, U.S. Foreign Policy Conference, Oct. 26–28, 1995. Muscatine, Iowa, The Stanley Foundation, 1995. Results of a symposium on the present and future of U.S.-Mexican relations.

6

The Middle East

✔ *What position should the U.S. take toward the new Likud government in Israel? Is a change in U.S. policy called for?*

✔ *Are the UN sanctions on Iraq working or not? Is it time to remove them?*

✔ *Should the U.S. lift the trade embargo on Iran?*

Basic Facts

	Israel[1]	Syria	Iraq	Iran
GDP (1994)	$71.1 billion	$28.1 billion (1993)	$18.5 billion	$59.8 billion
GDP per capita (1993)	$15,400 (1994)	$6,200	N/A	$2,230
Defense budget (1994)	$6.7 billion	$2.6 billion (1995)	$2.7 billion	$2.3 billion
Population (1995)	5.5 million[2]	14.7 million	20.6 million	61.3 million

[1] Excludes West Bank and Gaza.
[2] 82% Jewish, 14% Arab, 2% Christian, 2% Druze

Middle East ■ 63

- Israel and its Arab neighbors have fought five wars: Israel's war of independence (1948), the Suez war (1956), the Six-Day War (1967), the October war (1973) and the Israeli invasion of Lebanon (1982), as well as innumerable skirmishes.
- Israel receives $3 billion a year in U.S. foreign aid; Egypt receives $2.1 billion.
- 140,000 Jewish settlers live in the West Bank, Gaza, and East Jerusalem; 13,000 Jews live on the Golan Heights.
- Iraq's oil reserves are over 100 billion barrels, the world's second-largest reserves after Saudi Arabia.
- Iran's oil reserves are 93 billion barrels, and crude oil production accounts for 5.7% of the world total.

Background

Since World War II and the creation of the state of Israel in 1948, the Middle East has been a major focus of U.S. foreign policy. Central U.S. concerns have included:

- containing communism in the region;
- securing access to Persian Gulf oil; and
- supporting Israel's right to exist in peace with its Arab neighbors.

U.S. policy has also focused on combating terrorism and preventing the spread of weapons of mass destruction.

The Middle East has experienced great changes in the past five years: the end of the cold war and the collapse of the Soviet Union in 1991, Iraq's invasion of Kuwait and its defeat by a U.S.-led coalition in 1991, and dramatic progress in the Arab-Israeli peace process despite grave obstacles and setbacks. The containment of communism is no longer a factor in U.S. policy in the Middle East, but the other two concerns remain vital.

Successive U.S. Administrations have tried to broker peace settlements between Israel and its Arab neighbors. The U.S. played a central role in the historic Camp David talks in 1978 that led to a formal treaty between Israel and Egypt in 1979. On September 13, 1993, Presi-

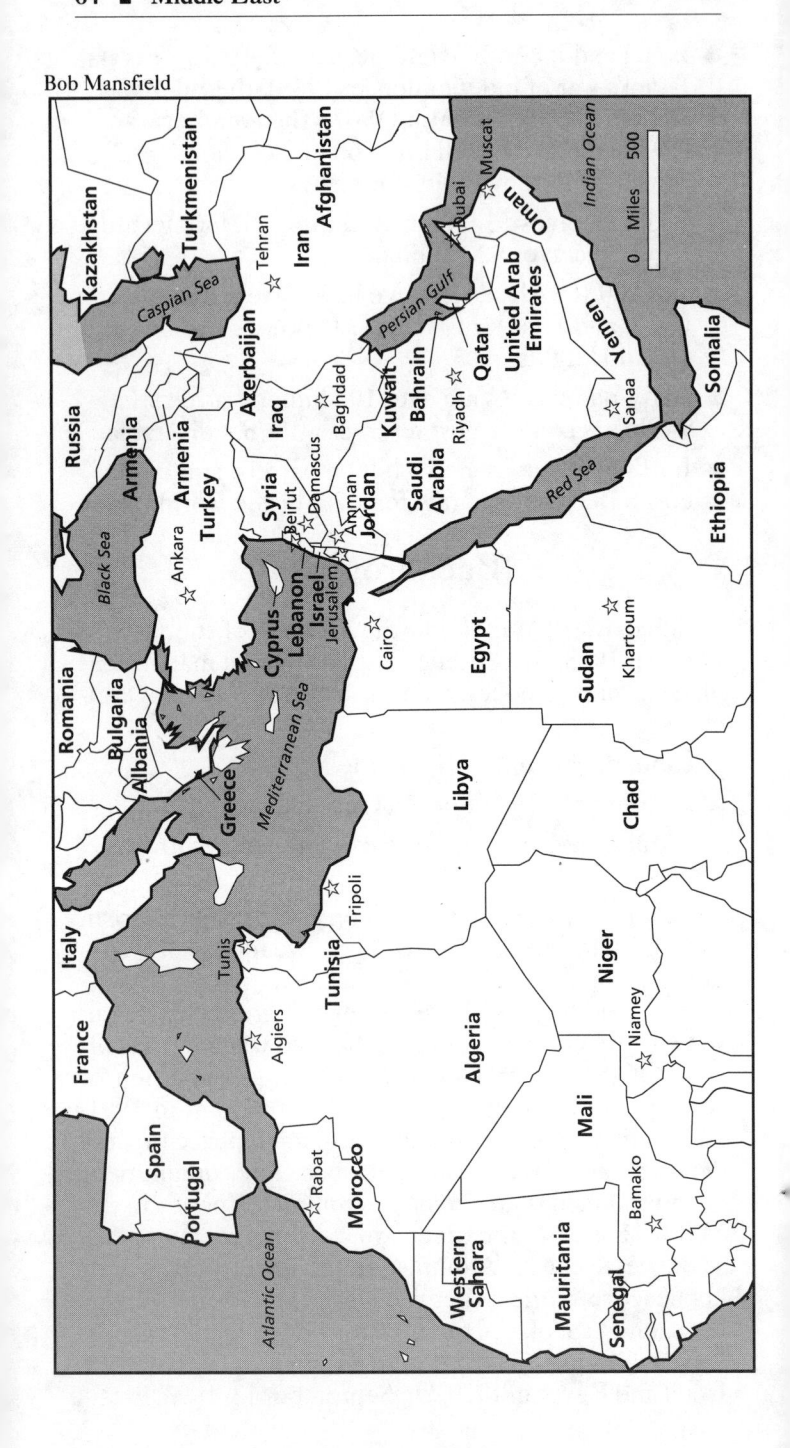

Middle East

Bob Mansfield

dent Bill Clinton presided over a dramatic handshake on the White House lawn between Yasir Arafat, leader of the Palestine Liberation Organization (PLO), and Israeli Prime Minister Yitzhak Rabin.

The Iran-Iraq War of 1980–88, touched off by Iraq's invasion of Iran, threatened the flow of oil throughout the Persian Gulf and underscored the region's strategic and economic importance. Two years after a tense peace was established, Iraq invaded and occupied oil-rich Kuwait in August 1990. The U.S. responded by organizing an international coalition of forces that drove Iraq from Kuwait in less than six weeks. By February 1991 Iraqi President Saddam Hussein's forces were routed. The 1991 war badly weakened Iraq, but Saddam remains in power despite comprehensive United Nations sanctions that have wreaked economic misery on his country. In May 1996, the UN partially lifted the sanctions: Iraq may sell up to $1 billion worth of oil every 90 days, under tight supervision, and use the money to buy food and medicine. International support for comprehensive sanctions is weakening due to the sentiment that the Iraqi people are being unfairly punished.

The UN discovered after the Persian Gulf war that Iraq secretly had built up a significant nuclear-weapons program, despite being a signatory to the Nuclear Nonproliferation Treaty (NPT) of 1968. Although Iraq had destroyed its nuclear-weapons capability under UN inspection by 1994, Iraq must still prove that all of its weapons of mass destruction, including chemical and biological weapons and missiles, are dismantled before the UN will fully lift the sanctions. According to UN inspectors, Iran, another party to the NPT, has no unexplained discrepancies in its nuclear programs. However, the U.S. believes that Iran wants nuclear weapons and may be able to produce them within 10 years. Most observers believe Israel has been an undeclared nuclear power since the 1970s but Israel will not confirm this. It is not a signatory to the NPT treaty.

Arab-Israeli Conflict

After World War II, Palestine, a former British mandate, was turned over to the UN, which passed a resolution in 1947 partitioning the land into independent Arab and Jewish states. War broke out and Israel declared itself a sovereign state on May 14, 1948. While the creation of Israel provided a home for the Jewish people, the war turned an estimated 600,000 to 760,000 Palestinians into refugees. They fled to Arab countries, including Jordan, Syria and Lebanon, and to the Gaza Strip. Many ended up in camps run by the UN.

The PLO was founded in 1964 and has been led since 1969 by Yasir Arafat.

In the 1967 Six-Day War, Israel seized the Sinai peninsula and the Gaza Strip from Egypt, the West Bank and East Jerusalem from Jordan, and the strategically important Golan Heights from Syria. UN Security Council Resolution 242 of November 1967 called on Israel to give up territories occupied in the war in return for Arabs' recognition of Israel's right to exist within secure boundaries. The "territory for peace" plan established the premise for peace negotiations.

In 1978, a great advance toward peace was made through the mediation of President Jimmy Carter by Egyptian President Anwar al-Sadat and Israeli Prime Minister Menachem Begin at Camp David, Md. The formal peace treaty, signed less than one year later, led Israel to return the Sinai to Egypt in 1982. The U.S. has provided large-scale aid to the two countries ever since and still participates in a multinational peacekeeping force in the Sinai.

The June 6, 1982, Israeli invasion of Lebanon was carried out to expel the PLO, depriving it of a base to make direct attacks on Israel. By September, Israel had driven the PLO from Beirut, the capital, and occupied southern Lebanon. However, Israel found itself mired in a civil war. After several failed peace attempts, Israel withdrew in 1985. Israel still occupies a nine-mile-wide "security zone" in southern Lebanon to protect its northern border. Some 40,000 Syrian troops are based in Lebanon.

In December 1987, mounting Palestinian frustration exploded in spontaneous demonstrations by rock-throwing youths in the occupied territories. The *intifada* (uprising) quickly developed into a revolt against Israeli rule. In a breakthrough one year later, Arafat explicitly recognized Israel's right to exist, accepted the UN's "territory for peace" premise for negotiations and renounced terrorism. The U.S. then recognized the PLO.

Progress in peace

The end of the cold war, the Iraqi defeat in the Persian Gulf war and the continuing intifada gave impetus to a new attempt at peacemaking. The groundwork was laid in Madrid, Spain, on October 30, 1991, when Israel and its Arab neighbors held the first direct negotiations since Camp David. The Madrid Conference established the foundation for future bilateral and multilateral talks to hammer out the details of the peace process.

The Labor party's return to power, led by Prime Minister Rabin, in June 1992 brightened the prospects for peace. Labor's leaders, unlike Likud's, were ready to exchange territory for peace. Secret negotiations in 1993 between Israel and the PLO in Oslo, Norway, led to the September 1993 signing of the landmark Declaration of Principles on Interim Self-Government and Arrangements. The declaration established a five-year plan for gradual Israeli transfer of the Gaza Strip and the city of Jericho to the control of a new Palestinian Authority (PA). After local Palestinian elections, negotiations for a permanent settlement were to begin. Although some deadlines were missed by parties on both sides of the negotiating table, the struggle for peace progressed. PLO and Israeli leaders apparently saw no alternatives.

In September 1995, Israel and the PLO agreed on terms for the second stage of interim Palestinian autonomy. These included an Israeli military pullback from Palestinian cities and villages in the West Bank with some two million inhabitants and the transfer of administrative authority to the PA as a prelude to elections for a Palestinian legislative council. The more daunting issues—the final status of Jerusalem, Jewish settlements, Palestinian refugees and the delineation of final borders between Israel and an as yet undetermined Palestinian political entity—were to be taken up no later than May 1996. (Negotiations were started but have not resumed since the Likud victory in the May elections.)

In January 1996, Arafat was elected president of the new autonomous PA by over 700,000 Palestinian voters in the Gaza Strip and West Bank. Three months later, Prime Minister Shimon Peres of the Labor party announced that Israel no longer ruled out the establishment of a Palestinian state, reversing a long-held Israeli government policy.

Obstacles to peace

Extremists on both sides have attempted to derail the peace process. On November 4, 1995, Prime Minister Rabin was assassinated by an Israeli opposed to peace with the Palestinians and, in early 1996, a wave of Islamic suicide bombers killed 59 Israelis. The terrorist attacks heightened Israeli citizens' fear for their personal security and brought into question the price of peace. Rabin's successor, former foreign and prime minister Peres, sealed off the Gaza Strip and the West Bank, preventing thousands of Palestinians from entering Israel. Talks between the PLO and Israel were suspended.

Leaders of 27 nations attended a one-day, U.S.-sponsored "Summit of the Peacemakers" in Egypt in March to condemn the terrorist bombings and vowed to cooperate in fighting terrorism and promoting peace. Syria and Lebanon did not attend the summit.

In April 1996, Hezbollah (Party of God), which operates with the implicit backing of the Syrian troops based in Lebanon, sent Katyusha rockets into northern Israel, spurring a massive air and artillery campaign in retaliation. Hundreds of thousands of Lebanese refugees fled to northern Lebanon. The situation worsened when Israel fired into a UN base for refugees in Lebanon on April 18, 1996, killing some 200 people, mostly women and children. The UN denounced the attack. With U.S. help, a cease-fire was reached on April 26, 1996.

The election of Benjamin (Bibi) Netanyahu, 46, on May 29, 1996, marked a turning point in the Arab-Israeli peace process. Netanyahu, leader of the Likud party, narrowly defeated Prime Minister Peres in Israel's first direct elections for prime minister. The election was akin to a referendum on the future course of the Arab-Israeli peace negotiations. Netanyahu won over 55% of the Jewish vote; Peres took almost 80% of the Arab vote. Netanyahu, a former army commando, wants to pursue a different, slower approach to the peace process to ensure a "secure peace." Although he claims he will not reverse the peace process, he has stated he would not accept the creation of a Palestinian state; would not withdraw Israeli troops from Hebron; would strengthen and encourage Jewish settlements in the West Bank; would not negotiate away the Golan to Syria; and would not discuss the status of Jerusalem.

Many in Israel, the Arab nations and the U.S. are concerned that the peace process will stop. Some fear Netanyahu's hard-line approach may set off a renewed cycle of Arab-Israeli violence. Others are more optimistic, noting that campaigning is quite different from governing. It was a Likud government that accepted "territory for peace" with Egypt and that began negotiations with the PLO in Madrid. Elie Wiesel, author and winner of the Nobel Peace prize, believes "no leader in Israel can simply stop the peace process; it is irreversible."

Israel-Syria relations

Any comprehensive peace settlement in the Middle East must include Syria, led by Hafez al-Assad since 1970. Syria is the last major Arab nation to remain in a state of war with Israel. Syria has insisted that Israel withdraw from the Golan Heights, which Israelis seized in 1967, as a precondition for negotiations.

With the loss of Soviet patronage, Assad realized he could not afford to continue Syria's costly confrontation with Israel, and in 1991 he entered into negotiations with it in Madrid. In 1994 Assad voiced his willingness to return to "normal, peaceful relations" if Israel returned the Golan Heights. A series of U.S.-mediated talks between Syria and Israel was held from mid-1995 to early 1996 in the U.S., raising hopes for a breakthrough. Before the wave of suicide bombs destroyed Peres's high standing in the polls, the former prime minister stated his readiness to return the Golan in exchange for peace, although only after a referendum.

The election of Netanyahu has cast a pall over the prospect of Syrian-Israeli peace. On June 3, 1996, Assad

Toles©The Buffalo News. Reprinted with permission of Universal Press Syndicate. All rights reserved.

stated he had no hope for the resumption of peace talks with Israel, adding that "things are not going ahead in a positive direction." Netanyahu has stated he will not exchange the Golan for peace for security reasons, but would negotiate "peace for peace." Without an Israeli-Syrian peace, there appears little hope for ending the violence between Israel and Lebanon, in effect a Syrian protectorate, let alone achieving a comprehensive Arab-Israeli peace.

Administration Policy

The U.S. has been a key mediator in Israeli-Arab negotiations. Secretary of State Warren Christopher has devoted much of his attention to the Middle East, traveling to the region over 20 times. U.S. mediation brought Israel and Syria to the negotiating table in 1995 and 1996. The U.S., however, still deems Syria a terrorist state for its sponsorship of terrorist groups such as Hezbollah in Lebanon. To further Israeli-Palestinian peace, the U.S. has pledged $500 million over a five-year period for the Palestinian Authority, one half of which had been disbursed by January 1996. The U.S. opposes any new West

Bank settlements. However, the Clinton Administration, like all previous Administrations, does not support an independent Palestinian state.

President Clinton openly backed Peres's reelection, signaling the U.S. preference for the Labor leader as the man to make peace. Before a winner was declared, Clinton stated that the U.S. "will continue its policy of support for the people of Israel, for the democratic process there, and for the process of peace." When the final tally was in, Clinton called to congratulate Netanyahu and invited him to the White House to discuss the future peace process. Secretary Christopher stated on June 2 that a more conservative leadership in Israel will require policy adjustments.

Persian Gulf policy

In May 1993, the U.S. announced a policy of dual containment for both Iraq and Iran. The policy relied on maintaining sanctions on Iraq and Iran and persuading other countries to harmonize their policies with those of the U.S., that is, denying Iraq and Iran aid, investment, credits and arms. The sanctions against Iraq were partially lifted in May 1996. In May 1995, U.S. concern about Iran's efforts to acquire weapons of mass destruction, foster terrorism and obstruct the Arab-Israeli peace process prompted the U.S. to impose a trade embargo on Iran. It failed to convince its allies to follow suit, and Europe and Japan continue to trade with Iran.

Arms proliferation concerns

Controlling the proliferation of weapons in the Middle East, the world's leading arms importer since the Vietnam War, is a top U.S. priority. To deny Iran a nuclear-weapons capability, the U.S. has heavily pressured other nations such as Russia and China to cancel new arms sales and deals to provide nuclear reactors, going so far as to share Washington intelligence on the Iranian nuclear program with Russian and Chinese officials. (Russia canceled the sale of machinery used to make weapons-grade material in May 1995, but, along with China, it did go through with a nuclear-reactor deal.)

Policy Options

1. **The U.S. should not change its policies toward the peace process due to Israel's new government.**
- **Yes:** The U.S. should stand firm and encourage Netanyahu to continue the peace process as his predecessors from the Labor party and the leaders of the PLO envisioned it. "Territory for peace" is the only way to have true peace in the Middle East.
- **No:** The U.S. should respect the policies adopted by Israel's democratically elected leadership. The U.S. must adapt to the new Likud government while continuing to seek peace.

2. **The U.S. should continue to cultivate relations with Syria.**
- **Yes:** Syria is the linchpin for a comprehensive peace settlement in the Middle East. Assad has come to the negotiating table and has stated his willingness to accept the "territory for peace" blueprint. Only by cultivating relations with Syria can the U.S. help broker peace in the Middle East and persuade Syria to renounce terrorism.
- **No:** Syria is a supporter of terrorism and should be isolated. Secretary Christopher has traveled to Syria over 20 times yet Syria continues to be an intractable player in the Middle East peace process. The U.S. should refuse to deal with Syria until it renounces terrorism.

3. **The U.S. should support lifting the UN sanctions on Iraq.**
- **Yes:** The sanctions have not led to the overthrow of Saddam Hussein but have brought economic hardship to the Iraqi people. The UN Security Council's partial lifting of sanctions in May 1996 was a step in the right direction.
- **No:** Iraq has not fully satisfied UN requirements for full disclosure to prove it has eliminated all weapons of mass destruction. Until it does so, the U.S. should press to keep sanctions in place.

4. **The U.S. should lift the trade embargo on Iran.**

❏ **Yes:** The trade embargo is not working because the U.S. does not have multilateral support: European countries and Japan continue to trade with Iran. While there still may be a need to contain Iran from a military point of view, the U.S. should try to engage Iran through commercial ties. The lifting of the trade embargo could be a reward for better behavior.

❏ **No:** The trade embargo has been successful in that it has led to a run on Iran's currency, discouraging other countries from extending credit or making investments in Iran. Also, Iran's efforts to develop weapons of mass destruction and to foster terrorism make it difficult for the U.S. to lift the sanctions and pursue a strategy of engagement. The U.S. must work to contain, not engage, such dangerous elements in the Middle East.

Select Bibliography

"The Future of U.S. Persian Gulf Strategy." Report of the Thirty-Sixth Strategy for Peace, U.S. Foreign Policy Conference, Oct. 26–28, 1995. Muscatine, Iowa, The Stanley Foundation, 1995. A diverse group of experts examines present and future U.S. policy options in the Persian Gulf region. Single copies available free from The Stanley Foundation, 216 Sycamore St., Suite 500, Muscatine, IA 52761-3831; Tel. (319) 264-1500.

"Measuring Successes and Continuing Negotiations in the Middle East." *U.S. Department of State Dispatch*, Feb. 12, 1996, pp. 38–40. Discussion of Middle East peace process and Persian Gulf security by Secretary of State Christopher, Israeli Prime Minister Peres and PLO Chairman Arafat.

"The Middle East." *Current History*, Jan. 1996. Entire issue devoted to the Arab-Israeli peace process, the U.S. role in the Middle East and the Persian Gulf states.

Potter, Lawrence G., "Middle East: Lasting Steps to Peace?" *Great Decisions 1995*, pp. 37–46. New York, Foreign Policy Association, 1995. Provides background of the Arab-Israeli conflict, nonpartisan analysis, U.S. policies and alternative options for the U.S.

7

Immigration

✔ *What criteria should be used to determine who is allowed into the U.S.?*

✔ *Does it pay to tighten border security?*

✔ *Should the U.S. provide health care and education to illegal immigrants?*

Basic Facts

- Proportion of U.S. population that was foreign-born in 1990: 7.9%
- Proportion of U.S. population that was foreign-born in 1910: 16%
- During the 1980s, more than half of the world's immigrants gained legal admission to the U.S.
- Estimated number of illegal immigrants who entered and remained in the U.S. in 1995: 300,000. Approximately half of these were visa overstayers.

Background

Over the last 200 years, U.S. policy on who should be allowed to immigrate has been shaped by public opinion, interest group pressures and foreign policy concerns.

Few attempts were made to control entry into the U.S. or to deal with immigrants once in the country until the 1870s. Beginning in the 1880s, public pressure led to increasingly restrictive legislation, including a series of Chinese Exclusion Acts; a prohibition on the importation of contract laborers (1885); the right to expel aliens (1888); knowledge of English as a requirement for naturalization (1906); and limits on Japanese immigration (1907).

The surge in immigration from Southern and Eastern Europe at the beginning of the 20th century led to calls for measures to reduce and restrict immigration from certain countries. The result was the National Origins Quota Act of 1924, creating immigration limits that reflected the ethnic background of the U.S. population in 1890 (changed to 1920 three years later).

Change in direction

World War II brought new foreign policy priorities, which in turn led to a relaxation of restrictions on some Asian immigration (China, India and the Philippines). Wartime labor shortages also produced some policy changes, especially the Bracero Program enacted by Congress in 1943 to bring Mexican agricultural workers into the U.S. under contract for specific time periods.

The McCarran-Walter Immigration and Nationality Act of 1952 consolidated the various laws covering immigration and naturalization (the process of becoming a citizen). Because it retained the national origins quota system, President Harry S. Truman vetoed it, but Congress overrode his veto.

Despite the efforts of Presidents Dwight D. Eisenhower and John F. Kennedy to discard McCarran-Walter's national-origins quota system and include provisions for refugees, it was not until 1965 that the 1952 Immigration and Nationality Act was substantially amended. The new act switched the emphasis from national origins, a policy that had favored northern Europeans, to family reunification—family members joining relatives. This gradually increased the proportion of Asian and Latin American immigrants coming to the U.S., although this result was not foreseen by the authors of the 1965 act. The 1965 legislation also established an overall annual limit of 290,000, with 6% reserved for refugees from Communist or Middle Eastern countries.

The Refugee Act of 1980 increased the number of refugees allowed to enter the U.S. from 17,400 to 50,000. It also expanded the refugee category to include those from anywhere, not just Communist countries and the Middle East.

In the Immigration Act of 1990, Congress raised the limit on legal immigration from around 500,000 to 700,000 annually, not including refugees. The bill also created the "diversity" visas, which were allocated by lottery to people from countries that were under-represented under the 1965 immigration system.

Illegal immigration

Concern about illegal immigration began to surface in the 1970s. Legislative solutions were attempted, but because of the lack of consensus on how to deal with illegal immigration nothing happened until the 1986 Immigration Reform and Control Act (IRCA). Its main provisions were amnesty for illegals who had entered the U.S. before January 1, 1982, and could prove continuous residence in the U.S. since that time; sanctions against employers who knowingly hired undocumented workers; and a Special Agricultural Worker (SAW) amnesty.

Immigration Trends
1820-1994

Year	Number of legal immigrants admitted to the U.S.	U.S. population
1820	8,385	9,638,453
1870	387,203	38,558,371
1910	1,041,570	92,228,496
1960	265,398	179,323,175
1980	530,639	226,542,203
1990	656,111*	248,709,873
1994	804,416	263,329,000

*An additional 880,372 people were given legal immigrant status under IRCA in 1990.

Bob Mansfield

Some 1.7 million applied for the general amnesty, and another 1.3 million for SAW amnesty, the latter more than double the highest estimate and apparently heavily subject to fraud. (Of the 3 million applications, 2.2 million were filed by Mexicans.) Some 2.7 million people qualified for the general amnesty. The newly legal residents began to petition to bring in their families, which has created an extremely large backlog in family members waiting to immigrate.

Employer sanctions

The employer-sanctions provisions of IRCA were intended to prevent the hiring of undocumented workers, thus removing employment as a prime incentive for coming to the U.S. Civil libertarians and representatives of some ethnic groups objected, claiming the sanctions would result in discrimination against all workers who looked "foreign." Businesses complained that it was difficult to verify if a worker's papers were valid, and many employers preferred to hire illegals, who would work for less pay than American citizens and in worse conditions. The federal government has spent little to enforce the employer sanctions part of the bill, and it is generally agreed that the IRCA provisions have not yet proved to be effective deterrents against illegal immigration.

Federal vs. state

Most immigrants settle in one of six states: California, New York, Texas, Florida, Illinois and New Jersey, with 25% going to California. California's high concentration of immigrants—both legal and illegal—combined with the state's sluggish economy resulted in the passage of Proposition 187 by voters in 1994. The aim was to deny publicly financed medical care and education to illegal immigrants. The legality of denying such services has been challenged in the courts, and Proposition 187 has yet to go into effect.

California and five other states have sued the federal government for reimbursement for the expenses incurred in providing services to illegal aliens.

Although there is general agreement that illegal aliens receive more in the way of public services than they

Martin Kozlowski©1996 by The New York Times Co.
Reprinted by permission.

pay in taxes, the situation of legal immigrants is more difficult to quantify. Some studies claim that legal immigrants cost U.S. taxpayers, while others suggest the opposite. In general, refugees and older immigrants use public services more than the average American, while other immigrants use them less. In spite of differences over the cost estimates, most agree that the federal government receives a disproportionate share of the taxes paid by legal immigrants, whereas local and state governments bear a disproportionate share of the costs for benefits such as education. Federal law and in some cases the Constitution forbid discrimination against those who are not citizens, which makes it difficult for the states to deny benefits.

Taking sides

Although immigration politics do not closely follow party lines, some Republicans have taken the lead in calling for restriction on the number of immigrants allowed into the U.S. However, there is division within the party on many aspects of overall immigration policies. For example, the libertarian wing of the party supports increased or even unlimited immigration, arguing that limits on immigration are tantamount to regulation of the workplace. There is also a split on whether to deny public education to children of illegal immigrants. Presidential candidate Bob Dole and California governor Pete Wilson support the ban, but some other prominent Republicans have expressed reservations.

Democrats, with their traditional support base of ethnic groups, tend to back liberal immigration policies. For example, President Clinton has said he would veto any legislation containing the education ban.

Proposals

The proposed legislation now being debated in Congress deals with

- ***Border security:*** Tightening security at U.S. borders is a priority for many lawmakers. Most of the expanded resources would go to increasing the number of Border Patrol agents from 4,500 to 10,000 and upgrading their equipment. Opponents question the cost of such programs and the potential for human-rights violations.

- ***Employer sanctions and verification of status:*** Allocating more resources to enforcement is under consideration. In addition, there is growing support for a national registry based on Social Security and immigration records that would enable employers to verify the status of job-seekers. Members of minority groups and civil libertarians object that a registry would discriminate against Hispanic and other job-seekers who looked "foreign," and would be prone to inaccuracies.

- ***States' burden:*** Although the six states suing the federal government for reimbursement for expenditures on illegal aliens are not expected to win, the government has made some attempts to help the states. Proposed anticrime legislation would make funds available to defray the costs of incarcerating illegal aliens. The Clinton Administration's proposed 1996 budget also includes funds to pay for some medical and education expenses for immigrants.

- ***Legal immigration:*** More and more lawmakers are calling for cutbacks in legal immigration, which exceeds 800,000 people a year. Some legislators propose lowering the ceiling to about 600,000. Others call for even bigger cuts, and some advocate a temporary moratorium on immigration.

Lawmakers have also proposed changing the priority system for legal admission. Family reunification currently accounts for over half of all legal immigration. Some proposals call for emphasizing employment skills, and others call for limiting family reunification to the immediate family, eliminating preferences currently given to siblings and adult children of citizens or legal permanent residents.

Other proposals include relaxing the rules on deportation and denying citizenship to children of illegal aliens born in this country.

In March, the House passed a major immigration bill that would tighten security along the border with Mexico, make illegal aliens ineligible for federal aid, and restrict the benefits available to legal aliens. The bill would also make it easier to refuse political asylum to foreigners claiming persecution but lacking documentation, and it would simplify deportation procedures. The legislation originally sought to restrict legal as well as illegal immigration, but the provisions on legal immigration were deleted in March.

The Senate decided to split the immigration legislation into two bills, one covering illegal immigration and the other, legal immigration. Because adjusting limits on legal immigration is extremely controversial, it is likely that no drastic changes will be made.

Push vs. pull

Immigration policy affects more than U.S. employers, employees and economic policy. The U.S. has traditionally been a safety valve for the unemployed south of the border. In weighing future policy on legal and illegal immigration, policymakers must take into account the effect on countries of origin of immigrants.

Administration Policy

The Clinton Administration has proposed substantial increases in the budget of the Immigration and Naturalization Service and simplification of the rules under which asylum claims are processed.

The Administration also supports stronger enforcement of employer sanctions to cut down on illegal immigration and development of a verification system, including some sort of national registry.

Immigrants by Major Category
Fiscal Year 1994

Family-related	461,725
Immediate relatives of citizens	(249,764)
Family preference	(211,961)
Employment preference	123,291
Refugee and asylee adjustments	121,434
Legalized aliens and relatives	40,096
Other	57,870
TOTAL	**804,416**

However, in the area of legal immigration the Administration has been walking a fine line between labor, which wants to cut down on the employment of immigrants who compete with U.S. citizens for jobs, and businesses, which want to be able to hire immigrants (legal ones, for high-tech jobs; illegal ones, for farm work and other unskilled jobs).

Policy Choices

Legal immigration

1. **Reduce the number of legal immigrants allowed into the U.S.**
- ❑ **Yes:** The U.S. cannot afford the social and economic costs presented by the annual admission of close to 1 million largely unskilled immigrants.
- ❑ **No:** New immigrants strengthen the country by increasing its cultural diversity, they perform jobs that others are unwilling to take, and their demand for goods and services expands the economy.

2. **Continue to give preference to immigrants with family ties, as opposed to immigrants with particular skills.**
- ❑ **Yes:** Family reunification is important for humanitarian reasons. In addition, immigrants who come in under this program have family members to vouch for them and are less likely to go on welfare.
- ❑ **No:** Giving preference to immigration of family members has led to a much higher number of en-

trants than was anticipated. As a result, there are now very large backlogs of people waiting to immigrate. And, the newcomers are often unskilled and uneducated and are apt to depend on welfare benefits.

3. **Reduce the number of refugees and asylum-seekers allowed to enter the U.S.**
- ❏ **Yes:** Statistics show that refugees are more likely to be on welfare than the general population or other legal immigrants.
- ❏ **No:** The U.S. should live up to its image as a champion of freedom and democracy by offering asylum to those fleeing political persecution.

Illegal immigration

1. **The U.S. should increase border security in order to keep out illegal immigrants.**
- ❏ **Yes:** This is a highly visible way of preventing illegal entry into the U.S., which has results that are easy to measure. A heightened security presence on the border also discourages people from attempting to cross.
- ❏ **No:** The border with Mexico is too long to be effectively sealed. When security is tightened in one place, border crossers switch to less secure areas.

2. **Enforce employer sanctions and set up a verification system.**
- ❏ **Yes:** The only way to cut down on the number of illegal immigrants in the U.S. is to prevent employers from hiring them. Setting up a registry of social security numbers for use by potential employers won't be any more intrusive than existing record keeping.
- ❏ **No:** Sanctions against employers who hire illegals is an unnecessary regulation of business. Also, a work-verification program could increase discrimination against members of minorities.

3. **Deny medical and education benefits to illegals.**
- ❏ **Yes:** Denying illegals access to free education and medical care will cut down on the number of illegals.

In addition, the burden for supplying these services falls disproportionately on a few states.

❑ **No:** Not providing health care to illegals could adversely affect the whole population, for example by causing tuberculosis to spread. Not allowing the children of illegals to attend school would create an underclass of illiterates, dependent on either crime or welfare.

Select Bibliography

Brimelow, Peter, *Alien Nation: Common Sense About America's Immigration Disaster.* New York, Random House, 1995. Senior editor of *Forbes* and *National Review* warns that immigrants threaten America's national identity, economy and environment, and he calls for the U.S. to shut its borders and restrict legal entry.

Fix, Michael, and Passel, Jeffrey S., *Immigration and Immigrants: Setting the Record Straight.* Washington, D.C., The Urban Institute, 1994. An attempt to provide a factual base and framework for discussion of immigration policy.

Rohan, Karen, "Immigration: An End to Open Doors?" *Great Decisions 1995.* pp. 69–78. New York, Foreign Policy Association, 1995. Examines the history of U.S. immigration policy and analyzes the current debate among the public and policymakers. Outlines Clinton Administration policy and provides alternative policy choices.

Teitelbaum, Michael S., and Weiner, Myron, eds., *Threatened Peoples, Threatened Borders: World Migration and U.S. Policy.* New York, Norton, 1995. Chapters on U.S. immigration policy compiled from an American Assembly conference at Columbia University.

Ungar, Sanford J., *Fresh Blood: The New American Immigrants.* New York, Simon & Schuster, 1995. Using interviews with immigrants and their families across America, the dean of the School of Communication at American University argues new immigrants are a positive force in the U.S.

8

Trade and the Economy

✔ *Should the U.S. continue to support free trade?*

✔ *Does trade cost American jobs?*

✔ *What trade policy best protects U.S. economic interests?*

✔ *Should the U.S. expand Nafta or get out?*

Basic Facts

- In 1970, trade accounted for 13% of the U.S. gross domestic product (GDP); by 1995, it accounted for 30%.
- U.S. exports have increased nearly 25% in two years; exports to nearly all U.S. major trade partners have grown.
- U.S. imports exceed exports, as they have every year but two since 1970.
- International trade provides jobs for 11 million Americans.
- Unemployment in the U.S. fell to 5.6% in 1995, the lowest level in six years.
- The actual average hourly wage for private non-agricultural workers decreased from $8.03/hr. in 1970 to $7.41/hr. in 1995 (1982 constant dollars).

Is trade good for the U.S.? How should the U.S. be pursuing trade with other nations?

Background

Protectionism vs. free trade

The basic principles of the U.S. free-trade system stem from the Great Depression. During the 1930s, nations tried to remedy their economic troubles by dramatically restricting trade with other nations. Economists generally agree that the U.S. trade restrictions imposed by the Hawley-Smoot Tariff Act of 1930 helped plunge the nation deeper into depression. As a result of that experience, the architects of the post–World War II trading system rejected protectionism in favor of free trade. In 1947, the leading industrialized countries set up a multinational institution, the General Agreement on Tariffs and Trade (GATT), dedicated to reducing trade barriers and resolving trade disputes.

The U.S. benefits from free trade and open foreign markets in three ways: (1) the sale of goods abroad brings jobs and profits to U.S. firms; (2) consumers have a wider choice of goods available at lower prices, e.g., Japanese tape players or French wines; and (3) competition from foreign trade puts pressure on U.S. firms to innovate and keep prices down. Japanese competition, for example, helped force Detroit automakers to make better and safer cars.

Not everyone, however, benefits from free trade. If, for example, Americans buy Japanese or German rather than American cars, Americans can lose their jobs. Job loss was a serious concern throughout America in 1996. In January U.S. corporations announced plans to lay off almost 100,000 workers, compared with the monthly rate of 37,000 in 1995. The issue of how trade affects U.S. jobs lies at the heart of the debate between free trade and protectionism.

U.S. jobs and wages

Those arguing for free trade maintain that the U.S. gains more jobs than it loses through trade and, furthermore, export-related jobs generally pay higher wages.

Heng/Cartoonists & Writers Syndicate

This is what President Bill Clinton refers to when he speaks of "good jobs at good wages."

Those arguing for protectionism believe that the American worker needs to be defended from nations trading unfairly and from U.S. firms moving overseas to take advantage of low wages. When such unfair conditions exist, they argue, free trade doesn't work. Protectionists argue further that the U.S. is losing quality manufacturing jobs to foreign competition, and the jobs that replace them are generally lower-wage jobs in the service sector.

A recent study by economists Jeffrey Sachs and Howard Shatz found that roughly 25% of the decline in U.S. wages over the past few years can be attributed to that small segment of U.S. manufacturing workers who are in competition with low-wage foreign workers. In the case of those workers, Sachs and Shatz argue, trade does affect wages.

U.S. wages have been stagnating since the 1970s, and most economists would argue that trade is a relatively minor factor. The majority of U.S. trade is conducted with partners that have wages similar to ours, namely Canada, Western Europe and Japan. Further, wage inequality has risen in industries not affected by trade.

Other factors that may be more significant causes of stagnation include the decline in union membership (union workers generally earn more than nonunion labor); fewer government social programs; the shift from manufacturing to service employment, which is generally lower paid; and, importantly, technological change.

There is a fair amount of consensus between the two major-party candidates, President Bill Clinton and former Senate Majority Leader Bob Dole (R-Kans.), over the importance of keeping an open trading system and abiding by U.S. trade agreements. But there are differences in how the U.S. should go about pursuing free trade—what institutions and instruments the U.S. should use.

Multilateralism vs. bilateralism

The multilateral trading system operates on the principle that free trade can best be protected and expanded if all trading nations operate under the same rules and reduce their trade barriers. There have been eight major rounds of negotiations, which have reduced tariff barriers to minimal levels. The latest round, the Uruguay Round, brought important types of trade under international regulations, including agricultural products, services and intellectual property rights (copyrights, for example). In addition, the Uruguay Round created a permanent institution, the World Trade Organization (WTO), to replace GATT. The WTO adopted many of the founding principles of GATT, but, in contrast to GATT, it can work continuously to initiate new negotiations and consider trade disputes between members; it does not have to wait for a new round of negotiations. The WTO began operations on January 1, 1995, with 76 members. It had 121 as of May 1996. Neither China nor Taiwan are members.

Critics of the multilateral trading system see the U.S. turning over too much authority to the WTO to rule on trade disputes. Republican presidential contender Patrick J. Buchanan called the WTO "a global supreme court of world trade, where for the first time the USA surrendered control of its trade policy to a world institution." Dole has also expressed concern about the WTO having the power to rule against the U.S. He proposed a WTO dispute-settlement review commission to examine all WTO rulings against the U.S. and set up a process for U.S. withdrawal from the organization.

The WTO's supporters, including the Clinton Administration, say it is a stronger organization than GATT that can bring better enforcement of international trade rules, which is to the U.S. advantage. They point out that no organization can force a change in U.S. laws; only the U.S. can legally do this.

In bilateral trade negotiations, the U.S. can set its own priorities and seek reductions in nontraditional trade barriers such as foreign customs and changes in business practices that are not covered by multilateral rules. For example, in Japan, local producers are traditionally favored over foreign manufacturers. Consequently, Japanese retail chains regularly buy from suppliers within the country without considering foreign goods. The disadvantage to focusing principally on bilateral negotiations is that the U.S. can appear to be a bully ganging up on weaker partners. Such a tactic can backfire and cause partners to retaliate against other U.S. products. Individual deals can simply be too time-consuming to be effective, whereas multilateral negotiations open up a market for a product to more than 100 countries simultaneously. On the other hand, achieving agreements through multilateral negotiations can also be frustrating and slow.

Increasingly, trade negotiations are being conducted by blocs of countries. Reducing trade barriers with geographic and ideological neighbors can be a stepping-stone to eventually bringing down these barriers on a multilateral basis.

Trading blocs

The drive to create free-trade areas among groups of neighboring countries has many origins, among them compelling political, social and economic reasons. Countries may want to stimulate greater trade and integration with their neighbors. After World War II ravaged Europe, the West Europeans envisioned a common "economic community" that would link their economies and later their political and social institutions and reduce the likelihood of future wars. There are three major trading blocs today.

■ *The European Union (EU)* is the oldest and most established bloc of trading nations that practice free trade among themselves. The EU is the most recent extension of a process of European integration that began with the creation of the Coal and Steel Community in 1952 and expanded in 1958 with the launching of the economic and atomic energy communities. Today, the 15-nation EU is an ever-growing union with the challenge of reaching out to new East European members and seeking to unite Europe under a common currency and monetary system. Critics argue that the EU has not always been a force for free trade outside the union and unfairly subsidizes a number of European products to the detriment of more-competitive foreign products.

■ *The North American Free Trade Agreement (Nafta)* between the U.S., Canada and Mexico was approved by the U.S. Congress in 1993 and created a free-trading arrangement for the first time between developed and developing nations. Nafta was particularly controversial in the U.S.: labor, environmental and other critics argued that the pact would send U.S. jobs to Mexico and increase pollution south of the border where environmental laws are laxer. Supporters contended Nafta would create a net job gain in the U.S., expand export markets for the U.S. and provide a more secure environment for investment.

While Nafta was supported by both the Republican (George Bush) and Democratic (Clinton) Administrations and a majority of the U.S. Congress, the controversy over the agreement continues today. In the first year the treaty was in effect (1994), the U.S. ran a $1.3 billion merchandise trade surplus with Mexico, showing gains as predicted by supporters. But the cheaper peso and Mexican economic woes reversed this trend in 1995, with the U.S. running a trade deficit with Mexico. The growing trade deficit with Mexico and concern about job losses in the U.S. have intensified the cry for repeal of the treaty by Nafta opponents. Both President Clinton and presidential candidate Dole, however, maintain the treaty continues to be in the U.S. interest and will produce gains in the long run. A drive to expand Nafta to include Chile was derailed in 1995 due to anti-free-trade sentiments in the Republican-dominated Congress.

■ *Asia-Pacific Economic Cooperation forum (APEC)* was established in 1989. Its 18 member nations border the Pacific ocean, from Japan, China and Southeast Asian countries, to Australia, the U.S., Canada, Mexico and Chile. With U.S. urging, APEC has set the goal of free trade and investment by the year 2020. Critics feel the organization's members are too diverse to be an effective bloc; they claim it is big on talk, short on accomplishments. Supporters argue APEC members represent the world's most dynamic trading nations and that the forum needs time to evolve.

There is speculation that some trading blocs may expand by adding new members and some may join forces. There is talk, for example, of a new trans-Atlantic free-trade agreement (Tafta) linking the European Union and North America. The Clinton Administration is committed to creating a comprehensive free-trade area with Latin America by the year 2005 in accordance with the agreement made by 34 hemispheric nations at the so-called Summit of the Americas held in Miami, Florida, in 1994.

Administration Policy

The Clinton Administration advocates open commerce and is committed to promoting trade relationships (multilateral, bilateral, bloc) to advance U.S. economic interests.

Signe/Cartoonists & Writers Syndicate

Two major trade accords completed during the Clinton Administration are Nafta and the multinational agreement creating the WTO. The 1994 Summit of the Americas free-trade goal deepened the earlier commitment of the Bush Administration. The Clinton Administration also helped persuade the APEC nations to adopt free trade as their goal for the coming decade.

Supporters point out that this Administration has been more forceful than its predecessor in using retaliation and the threat of sanctions, such as on Japanese luxury cars, when U.S. trading partners do not live up to agreements. These confrontational tactics have succeeded in wresting concessions from U.S. trading partners. Critics contend that the Administration has done little to stop the growing surge of protectionism in the country. *Newsweek* writer Marc Levinson argues in the March/April 1996 issue of *Foreign Affairs* that the Clinton Administration, in fact, has fanned the flames of rising protectionism by overselling trade as a way to achieve good jobs at good wages. The erosion of the long-standing pro-trade coalition on Capitol Hill, Levinson maintains, was dramatized by the Administration's loss of fast-track authority (which assures that Congress votes within 90 legislative days and cannot amend a trade bill) for Chile.

Policy Choices

1. **The U.S. should continue to promote free trade by supporting the WTO.**
- ❏ **Yes.** Only by pursuing the expansion of free trade through multilateral means can the U.S. ensure that nations do not slip backward to protectionism, as happened in the 1930s. U.S. sovereignty is well protected in the WTO: the U.S., as the largest economy, has the major voice, and the WTO cannot change U.S. laws, such as altering environmental standards, without U.S. consent.
- ❏ **No.** The U.S. has surrendered too much sovereignty to an international organization where it has only one vote. The U.S. must protect its own interests without turning over decisionmaking to foreign bureaucrats.

2. To save American jobs, the U.S. should impose greater trade restrictions on foreign products.

❏ **Yes.** The U.S. should restrict imports from unfair traders who are running big trade deficits with the U.S., like Japan and China. U.S. workers are losing jobs unfairly to countries that subsidize their products and pay workers paltry salaries.

❏ **No.** Imposing trade restrictions will ultimately cost more American jobs than it saves. Hundreds of thousands of jobs depend on U.S. exports; these are good jobs at good wages. Those who lose their jobs should be retrained for better ones.

3. The U.S. should continue to support Nafta and extend it to include other Latin American trading partners.

❏ **Yes.** Free trade with our neighbors is still in our economic and political interest. Mexico and all of Latin America represent a huge export market. The U.S. should not be short-sighted and focus only on Mexico's current crisis but should consider the potential for even more jobs and greater prosperity for our country that comes from continuing and expanding Nafta.

❏ **No.** Nafta was a bad deal for the U.S. and supporters' claims of its benefits have not held true—the trade deficit with Mexico has increased and immigration has gone up. The U.S. cannot compete with low-wage countries where environmental laws and democratic practices are not implemented. If Nafta created a bad deal with Mexico, expanding it would only compound the economic losses to the U.S.

Select Bibliography

Grayson, George W., "The North American Free Trade Agreement." *Headline Series* No. 299. New York, Foreign Policy Association, 1993. An overview of the origins, politics and content of Nafta—with a discussion of the prospects for the accord's impact on Mexico, the U.S. and bilateral relations.

Kantor, Mickey, "Testimony before the House Ways and Means Trade Subcommittee," Mar. 13, 1996. Available free from the Public Affairs Office of the U.S. Trade Representative, 600 17th St. N.W., Washington, D.C. 20508; Tel. (202) 395-3230. Provides an overview of Administration trade policy and, in particular, Administration arguments and defense of U.S. sovereignty under the WTO.

Noland, Marcus, "Economic Cooperation in the Asia-Pacific: Openings for the U.S.?" *Great Decisions 1996*, pp. 33–41. New York, Foreign Policy Association, 1996. Reprint of the article available free from the Foreign Policy Association, 470 Park Avenue So., New York, N.Y. 10016; Tel: (800) 477-5836. Analyzes the Asia-Pacific region's economic growth and integration and implications for the U.S.

Richardson, J. David, and Rindal, Karin, *Why Exports Matter: More!* Washington, D.C., Institute for International Economics and The Manufacturing Institute, Feb. 1996. Available for $25 plus $2.95 s&h from the National Association of Manufacturers, Suite 1500-North Tower, 1331 Pennsylvania Ave. N.W., Washington, D.C. 20004; Tel. (800) 637-3005. This study rebuts claims that international trade hurts jobs and wages by showing higher wages, productivity and growth rates for firms that export.

Weintraub, Sidney, *Nafta: What Comes Next?* New York, Praeger, 1994. Argues that deepening Nafta (getting Nafta provisions more thoroughly implemented) may be more advisable than widening Nafta (extending it to other countries).

9

The U.S. Role in the UN

✔ *Should the U.S. take a leadership role (troops, logistics, funding) in UN peacekeeping operations?*

✔ *Should U.S. troops serve under foreign command in UN peacekeeping operations?*

✔ *Does the UN have the right to intervene in the internal affairs of sovereign nations, e.g., to provide humanitarian aid?*

✔ *Should the U.S. withhold its dues to influence UN reform?*

Basic Facts

- The UN Charter was signed in San Francisco on June 26, 1945; it came into force on October 24, 1945.
- 51 original member states; there are currently 185.
- Principal organs: the General Assembly, where every member has one vote, the Security Council, with five permanent members (Britain, China, France, Russia and the U.S.), the Economic and Social Council, the International Court of Justice, and the Secretariat. The secretary-general is

Boutros Boutros-Ghali of Egypt, whose five-year term expires in 1996.

- UN specialized agencies include the World Bank, the World Health Organization (WHO), the Food and Agriculture Organization (FAO), and the International Labor Organization (ILO).
- The UN's annual operating budget: $1.3 billion. The U.S. share is approximately $321 million. The U.S. owes $1.5 billion, including some $900 million for peacekeeping.
- The top six financial contributors to the UN are the U.S. (25%), Japan (14.8%), Germany (9%), France (6.4%), Britain (5.3%) and Russia (5%). Collectively, these states account for more than 65% of the regular UN budget.
- UN peacekeeping operations cost $3 billion in 1995. The budget for 1996 is $1.3 billion.

Background

The UN serves as the preeminent international forum where countries can air their differences within an accepted framework of rules. The UN has four distinct roles:

1. The UN promotes collective security. It has the authority to settle disputes between nations and address threats to international peace. It can help unify countries against a common international danger, such as Iraq's invasion of Kuwait, and help settle local and internal conflicts, such as those in the former Yugoslavia, Angola, Mozambique, Cambodia and El Salvador.
2. The UN provides concerted economic development assistance.
3. The UN helps safeguard human rights and promote democratic values and the rule of law.
4. The UN can act as a primary coordinator on issues that transcend national boundaries, such as disarmament and arms control, international terrorism

and narcotics, global health and social development, and the environment.

For the first 45 years of the UN's existence, the East-West confrontation overshadowed the UN's deliberations and actions. The collapse of the Soviet Union and the end of the cold war (1989–91) transformed relationships between countries and changed the UN's priorities. As fears of an East-West nuclear confrontation eased, the world body's attention shifted to the rash of regional and local conflicts and the greatly increased demands for UN intervention.

While Central America's civil wars wound down and wars that had claimed hundreds of thousands of lives in Ethiopia, Eritrea and Mozambique ended, other conflicts erupted in Bosnia and Herzegovina, Nagorno-Karabakh, Somalia and Rwanda, and civil wars persist in Sri Lanka, Liberia and Afghanistan. The conflicts in Somalia and Rwanda became humanitarian catastrophes, prompting large-scale international intervention. The intensity of the fighting displaced millions of persons, overwhelming UN agencies, international humanitarian organizations and the resources of the countries where the refugees fled.

UN peacekeeping

Although the term "peacekeeping" does not appear in the text of the UN Charter, the UN mounted its first peacekeeping operation three years after its founding. Peacekeeping grew out of the UN's authority to settle disputes and address threats to peace under Chapters VI and VII of its Charter.

From 1945 to 1990, the UN approved 18 peace operations; after 1990, the UN initiated 23 new operations. Today there are 16 UN peace operations around the world (see map).

These fall into three general categories:

- peace-enforcement missions to deliver aid and protect civilians;
- traditional peacekeeping operations to implement specific nation-building duties; and
- military observer forces to supervise predetermined truces or cease-fires. Their mandates are generally

broad and include nation-building responsibilities, such as election monitoring or assisting transitional governments.

The peacekeeping operations range from observer missions in buffer zones, consisting of noncombatant troops, to more volatile peace-enforcement operations that rely on combat troops to separate belligerents.

■ *U.S. Role:* During the cold war, U.S. participation in UN peacekeeping consisted primarily of financial and logistical support, since the involvement of U.S. or Soviet troops would have called into question the impartiality of the force. In recent years, Presidents Ronald Reagan, George Bush and Bill Clinton have supported in principle—though not necessarily with troops or funds—UN peace operations.

Since the deaths of 18 American soldiers in Somalia in 1993, popular and congressional opposition to U.S. involvement in UN peacekeeping has grown. In 1994 Clinton issued a Presidential Decision Directive on peace operations designed to impose more discipline on UN and U.S. peacekeeping efforts. The directive calls for a more selective U.S. role in peace operations, a reduction in costs, and clarification of policy regarding command and control of U.S. forces. It also outlines reforms for the management of UN peacekeeping. Some members of the military are concerned that U.S. commitments to UN peacekeeping harm U.S. military capability and readiness to address primary U.S. security interests.

■ *Humanitarian Emergencies:* Recent international conflicts have affected an unprecedented number of civilians. Civilian noncombatant casualties have dramatically increased. Some specialists attribute this to the deliberate targeting of civilians because of their ethnic or religious affiliation. As a direct consequence of these conflicts, there are some 27 million refugees—10 million more than five years ago.

Recent crises have thrust the UN into war-ravaged societies where belligerents are often indifferent to the most basic humanitarian principles. Consequently, the UN must try to address the victims' immediate needs while simultaneously attempting to work with and reconcile the warring parties. Where there are rapid and

[Cartoon by Danziger, The Christian Science Monitor: "UN peacekeeping troops enter the world's newest hot spot - the US Congress."]

Danziger©*The Christian Science Monitor*

mass population movements, it is all the harder for the UN to mobilize and deploy enough resources quickly to meet the refugees' needs.

The UN faces many obstacles in addressing humanitarian crises. Often its capacity to provide protection and assistance is undermined by an absence of law and order. Relief workers are often subject to manipulation by the belligerents. At times, one party will disrupt or divert relief supplies to gain political leverage. These problems have occurred frequently in the Bosnia and Herzegovina and Rwanda conflicts. Further, relief workers' access, often under dire conditions, to emergency areas is frequently dependent on hastily brokered agreements. The lack of support from member countries hampers the UN's ability to deal with long-term needs. UN members' political attitudes toward a particular crisis, their strategic interests in specific areas, and media attention often shape the UN's response.

UN reform

Critics have called the UN and its agencies wasteful, fraudulent, overstaffed and mismanaged. The UN has taken a number of steps to improve its operations. For the first time, in 1996 the UN has a no-growth budget; over the next two years it plans to cut its worldwide staff by 10%. A UN inspector general has been appointed to crack down on fraud and waste, and responsibility for management reform has been assigned to an American under-secretary general, a former CEO of Price-Waterhouse. A UN high-level working group on reform is developing a blueprint for the organization for the 21st century.

■ *U.S. Initiatives:* The U.S. has taken steps to induce reform of the UN's administration and management. Armed with the 1985 Kassebaum Amendment (Senator Nancy Kassebaum, R-Kans.), the U.S. in the 1980s threatened to cut its annual contribution to the UN operating budget unless the UN introduced a weighted voting system on fiscal matters. In 1994, Congress passed the Pressler Amendment (Senator Larry Pressler, R-S.D.), which called for the UN to establish an independent inspector general's office or face the withholding of a sizeable percentage of U.S. contributions. This initiative culminated in the establishment of an Office of Internal Oversight in the UN Secretariat.

Current Policy

■ *Budget and Finances:* In early 1996 the UN faced the worst cash-flow crisis in its history and the possibility it would run out of money before the end of the year. Since May, the UN has been borrowing cash set aside for peacekeeping to pay daily operating expenses. The budget crisis is due to the delay of the U.S. and other member countries in paying assessed dues, both for the regular budget and for peacekeeping operations. As of April 1996, member countries owed back-payments totaling $2.8 billion.

The U.S. owes the UN nearly half of all late payments. In 1995, the U.S. paid 12% (instead of 25%) of the UN budget; this year it is paying less than 12%. Failure to pay its arrears in violation of its treaty obligations could cost the U.S. the loss of voting rights in the General Assembly.

The U.S. is asking UN members to reduce the U.S. share of the UN regular budget to 20%. This would mean a reduction in the peacekeeping assessment rate from 31% to no more than 25%.

The Clinton Administration has proposed to Congress a five-year plan for paying off its debts to the UN, with actual payments tied to UN reforms, a leaner budget and additional cuts in the Secretariat staff. Negotiations between the White House and bipartisan congressional staffs have stalled over differences on the nature of reforms.

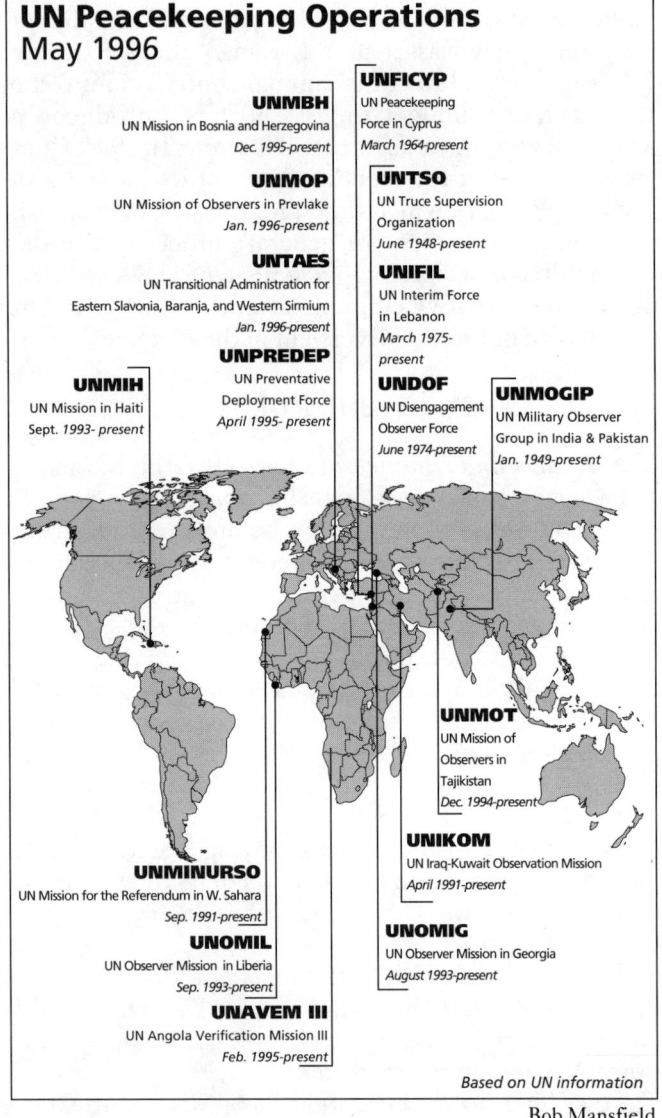

UN Peacekeeping Operations
May 1996

UNMBH
UN Mission in Bosnia and Herzegovina
Dec. 1995-present

UNMOP
UN Mission of Observers in Prevlake
Jan. 1996-present

UNTAES
UN Transitional Administration for Eastern Slavonia, Baranja, and Western Sirmium
Jan. 1996-present

UNMIH
UN Mission in Haiti
Sept. 1993- present

UNPREDEP
UN Preventative Deployment Force
April 1995- present

UNFICYP
UN Peacekeeping Force in Cyprus
March 1964-present

UNTSO
UN Truce Supervision Organization
June 1948-present

UNIFIL
UN Interim Force in Lebanon
March 1975-present

UNDOF
UN Disengagement Observer Force
June 1974-present

UNMOGIP
UN Military Observer Group in India & Pakistan
Jan. 1949-present

UNMOT
UN Mission of Observers in Tajikistan
Dec. 1994-present

UNIKOM
UN Iraq-Kuwait Observation Mission
April 1991-present

UNOMIG
UN Observer Mission in Georgia
August 1993-present

UNMINURSO
UN Mission for the Referendum in W. Sahara
Sep. 1991-present

UNOMIL
UN Observer Mission in Liberia
Sep. 1993-present

UNAVEM III
UN Angola Verification Mission III
Feb. 1995-present

Based on UN information

Bob Mansfield

The Administration and a majority in Congress support the overall mission of the UN. They consider it generally a good investment, especially for relieving the U.S. from shouldering the role of world policeman. Nevertheless, as part of the drive to reduce the federal deficit, the Republican-controlled Congress cut U.S. funding to the UN in 1995 and reduced Clinton's budget for 1996 UN peace operations. Congress did approve in April 1996 $304 million in overdue payments for the UN's 1995 operating expenses and $359 million in peacekeeping contributions, of which $313 million has already been paid.

Some congressmen oppose U.S. participation in UN peacekeeping operations on the grounds that U.S. troops should not serve under foreign command. Opponents call this a nonissue: Americans attached to UN peacekeeping operations serve under U.S. commanders.

In October 1995 Representative Joe Scarborough (R-Fla.) introduced a bill calling for U.S. withdrawal from the UN within four years. Cosponsors include House Majority Whip Tom DeLay (R-Tex.) and Deputy Majority Whip John Doolittle (R-Cal.). The sponsors reject "Wilsonian internationalism" and state that U.S. participation is more costly than it is worth.

Former Senate Majority Leader and Republican presidential candidate Bob Dole supports the overall mission of the UN but opposes giving the UN greater autonomy.

Policy Choices

1. The U.S. and the UN

❏ **a.** Give full U.S. support to strengthening the UN's ability to resolve conflicts, alleviate humanitarian crises and promote development.

OR

❏ **b.** Rely on U.S. unilateral military action to resolve conflicts while encouraging the UN to concentrate on alleviating humanitarian crises and promoting development.

OR

❏ **c.** Withdraw from the UN.

2. **The U.S. and Peacekeeping**
- ❏ a. Send U.S. troops and make financial contributions on a selective basis where U.S. vital interests are at stake.
OR
- ❏ b. Provide logistical and financial support and troops for UN peacekeeping operations wherever they are needed.
OR
- ❏ c. Decline to participate in future UN peacekeeping missions.

3. **The U.S. and UN Reform and Finances**
- ❏ a. Continue to withhold past and present assessments in order to put pressure on the UN to reform.
OR
- ❏ b. Pay all past and present dues in full so that the UN can continue to function.

Select Bibliography

Albright, Madeleine K., "The UN: What's in It for the U.S.?" *U.S. Department of State Dispatch*, Mar. 11, 1996, pp. 104–6. The U.S. representative to the UN presents the case for continued U.S. participation in the UN.

Carlsson, Ingvar, "The UN at 50: A Time to Reform." *Foreign Policy*, Fall 1995, pp. 3–18. Survey of UN reform proposals and policies.

Carroll, Raymond, "United Nations at 50." *Great Decisions 1995*, pp. 3–12. New York, Foreign Policy Association, 1995. A nonpartisan look at the UN and Boutros Boutros-Ghali's vision of its future.

Picco, Giandomenico, "The UN and the Use of Force." *Foreign Affairs*, Sept./Oct. 1994, pp. 14–18. Survey of the secretary-general and Security Council roles.

Touval, Saadia, "Why the UN Fails." *Foreign Affairs*, Sept./Oct. 1994, pp. 44–57. Discussion of the problems and limitations of the UN.

Weiss, Thomas G., "The United Nations at Fifty: Recent Lessons." *Current History*, May 1995, pp. 223–28. Overview of UN intervention successes and failures and reform proposals.

10

Defense and Security

✔ *Given a relatively limited budget, what priorities should head the post-cold-war defense agenda?*

✔ *How urgent is a nationwide missile defense system?*

✔ *Should the U.S. give defense dollars to former Soviet states and North Korea to 'cork the nuclear genie'?*

✔ *Is the nation too involved in peacekeeping missions?*

Basic Facts

Thanks to the abrupt collapse of the Soviet Union in 1991, the U.S. is the sole surviving military superpower. Today, no single overwhelming threat challenges this armed American might. Pentagon planners under Presidents George Bush and Bill Clinton thus enacted significant cuts in their forces and budgets. Although not cutting deep enough for those hoping for a large "peace dividend," these reductions would have been unthinkable when the U.S.-Soviet arms race still raged:

■ In 1988, Washington maintained close to 325,000 troops in Europe; today, only 100,000 remain—with

a similar number stationed in the Asia-Pacific region.
- Overall active-duty troop numbers will continue to fall, from just under 2.1 million in 1990 to just over 1.4 million by 1999, with a concomitant reduction in divisions, air wings and so on.
- Long-range, strategic nuclear stockpiles are shrinking to 3,000–3,500 deliverable warheads, less than a third of their cold-war numbers.
- Since 1990, the total value of Defense Department spending has fallen by 27% (see graph on p. 109). President Clinton in March requested $243 billion for the Pentagon in fiscal year (FY) 1997.

Background

In light of the dramatic evolution of the national security environment over the past half decade, bitter partisan disputes over military policy have played a smaller role in the 1996 presidential campaign thus far than in the recent past. The principal militarily significant areas of debate between a Republican Congress and a Democratic White House concern (1) the Clinton Pentagon's military strategy; (2) the relative areas of emphasis in a reduced Pentagon budget—e.g., the Clinton stress on immediate troop readiness versus the Republican push for long-range hardware modernization; (3) the advisability of erecting systems to defend the continental U.S. from missile attack; (4) the details of policies designed to stem nuclear proliferation; and (5) assigning U.S. troops to peacekeeping duties in far-flung trouble spots.

Paying for two wars and new weapons

In late 1993, the Pentagon wound up its so-called Bottom-Up Review (BUR) of post-cold-war defense needs. Compared to the Bush Administration's "Base Force," which called for 12 active-duty Army divisions, 12 aircraft-carrier battle groups and 14 Air Force fighter wings, the BUR allows for 10 divisions, 11 carriers and 13 wings. The BUR also insists that the military be able to wage two near-simultaneous "major regional con-

By Gamble for the Florida Times-Union.
Reprinted with special permission of King Features Syndicate.

flicts." The improbability that the Clinton force could sustain that burden, and the equal unlikelihood that it would ever have to, are subjects of heated debate. More pressing is the issue of the adequacy of projected Pentagon budgets to pay for the BUR's battalions.

In their "Contract with America," Republicans who won control of the House of Representatives in 1994 called for a revitalized defense. They have made much of a 1994 finding by the General Accounting Office, the investigative arm of Congress, that the Pentagon could fall more than $150 billion short of meeting needs through the end of the decade. The most difficult problem, it seems, will be paying for a costly new round of hardware modernization, the bills for which will be coming in around the turn of the century. The Air Force's planned F-22 stealth fighter fleet, to cite just one project, will run to some $73.5 billion.

In its budget resolution in 1995, the Republican Congress voted to boost projected defense spending from 1997 to 2002 by $13 billion over the figures planned by Clinton. In his latest budget proposal, however, Clinton foresees spending $30.5 billion more during those years than he did last year. But spending on procurement (i.e., modernization) would continue its roughly 70% decline over the past decade, sloping upward only in FY 1998. Meanwhile, immediate troop readiness—pay raises and ample funding for recruitment, retention of quality troops and training exercises—continues to receive unprecedented dollars and attention.

Many analysts view this era of unchallenged U.S. military supremacy as an opportunity to invest in future weapons and tactics. But slicing into the traditional Democratic Achilles' heel of being "weak on defense," Republican critics have attacked Clinton for alleged shortfalls in immediate readiness. Defense Secretary William J. Perry has thus pledged "to make readiness the first priority, even at the expense of other important uses for the department's resources." The Republican Congress has also tended toward a short-term view. Lawmakers have earmarked additional funds for current-generation weapons that the Pentagon says it has enough of—such as the B-2 stealth bomber, which costs about $1 billion—or for expansive new procurement projects that are likely to widen the fiscal "plans/funding mismatch" downstream.

When reducing the federal budget deficit tops the political agenda, the prospects for significant defense budget growth are slim. Either troop numbers will have to be further reduced, costly readiness initiatives relaxed or modernization plans scaled back. Republican politicians are themselves sharply divided between "defense hawks" and "deficit hawks," but deficit reduction seems to be the watchword of the day. Whoever wins the White House in November, a dramatic expansion (or reduction) of defense budgets seems unlikely.

Defending against ballistic missiles

Thirteen years and some $40 billion in Pentagon research spending after President Ronald Reagan delivered his "Star Wars" speech proposing to render strategic nuclear weapons "impotent and obsolete," the wisdom of building a ballistic missile defense (BMD) network capable of knocking incoming missiles out of the skies over America is a fixture of U.S. strategic debate.

The Democratic go-slow school has prevailed. America remains an adherent to the Anti-Ballistic Missile (ABM) Treaty of 1972, which sharply limits the nationwide BMD systems the U.S. and Russia are allowed to deploy. Missile defense proponents argue that the 1972 treaty merely ensures continued U.S. vulnerability to attack. Treaty proponents respond that restraining defenses is the only way to ensure fulfillment of the two strategic arms reduction treaties (Start I and II), which will sharply slice into U.S. and Russian nuclear stockpiles.

Under the Clinton Administration, the Pentagon is focused largely on developing devices that can knock down tactical ballistic missiles with a range of 600 miles or less. Last year, the Republican Congress boosted the Administration's proposed spending for BMD (from $2.9 billion to $3.4 billion), and directed that some sort of *national* missile defense system be built by 2003. Early in 1996, however, the Pentagon chose to reemphasize antitactical missile weapons, while de-emphasizing work on arms that have potential against longer-range missiles. The Administration also rejects the 2003 deadline. Instead it would devise a national BMD system over the next three years that could be fielded within another three years, but only if the threat warrants doing so.

The actual requirements for a nationwide missile defense are in dispute. The U.S. intelligence community predicted in late 1995 that "rogue states," such as Iran, North Korea or Libya, would be unable to develop a missile that could reach the U.S. within the next 15 years. But proponents of a nationwide BMD network, including many Republican lawmakers, remain convinced that it is a necessity.

Corking the nuclear genie

Spending on "nontraditional defense" programs—some $5 billion a year on environmental cleanup and compliance programs and the roughly $400 million per year spent on "Cooperative Threat Reduction" assistance for the dismantling of the nuclear weapons in the former Soviet states—has become a target for Republican critics. Last year, House Republicans moved to rescind a $110 million project to provide U.S.-built housing units for Russian officers stationed at missile bases that are being shut down. U.S. dollars are also being used to buy up and secure Russian uranium and to provide nonthreatening work for Russian atomic scientists.

The Chairman of the Joint Chiefs of Staff has defended this program as "a very good investment for the military." More-hawkish politicians view it as a subsidy for not always friendly Russian leaders.

Similar controversy surrounds a 1994 agreement with North Korea, under which that state would abandon its nuclear-weapons development effort in exchange for energy subsidies and help in building two nonmilitary nuclear-power reactors. The agreement extends into the next century. Most of the costs will be borne by Japan and South Korea; U.S. expenses are pegged at about $30 million a year. Conservatives have disparaged this approach as "life support for [North Korea's] repressive Communist regime." Administration supporters defend the pact as the safest way of diverting a heavily armed regime from goals that imperil Northeast Asian stability.

The Indo-Pakistani atomic arms race appears to be heating up, while Iran, Iraq and a handful of other nations are likely to keep seeking a nuclear capability. The threat of nuclear proliferation will continue to confront the U.S.

Green helmets or blue helmets?

Far fewer U.S. troops may be quartered overseas, but those who remain have seen more action in more places in the past five years than during any comparable period in the four-decade cold war. Most of this activity has taken place in peacekeeping or policing operations. In 1994–95, almost 120,000 Americans served in 16 separate "contingency operations" in Haiti, the former Yugoslavia, Rwanda and elsewhere. At the beginning of 1996, 20,000 U.S. troops were sent to enforce a shaky peace in Bosnia.

Distrustful of the UN, under whose aegis many of these missions have been mounted, Republicans tend to view peacekeeping as a diversion of U.S. military energy (and a waste of dollars and lives) on tasks with no immediate bearing on U.S. national interests. No less contentious is the question of placing U.S. troops under foreign command in multilateral operations. In the face of a Republican-led drive last year to curtail presidential power to field peacekeepers, Clinton issued a policy stressing that he "will never relinquish command

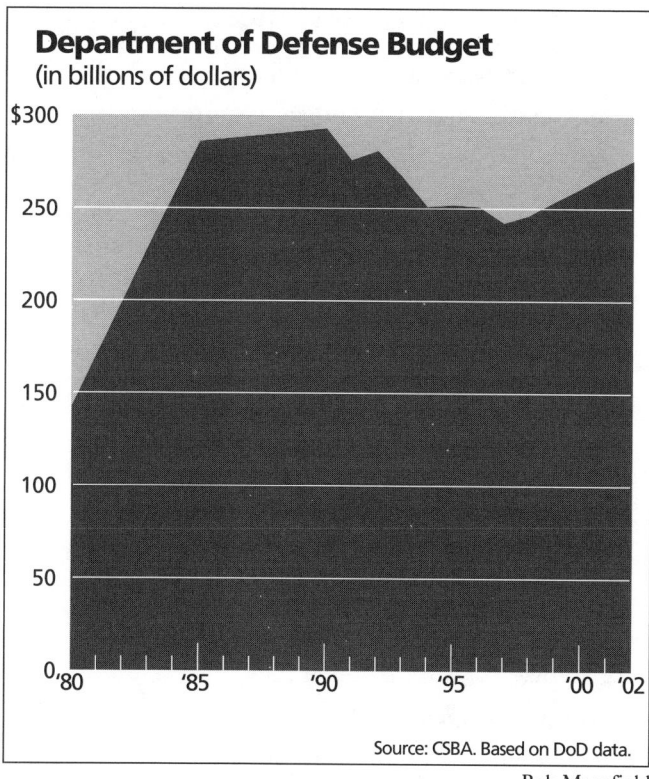

Department of Defense Budget
(in billions of dollars)

Source: CSBA. Based on DoD data.

Bob Mansfield

of U.S. forces," but, as commander in chief, he "has the authority to place U.S. forces under the operational control of a foreign commander when doing so serves American security interests." The Army's discharge in January of a Persian Gulf war veteran who refused to wear the blue UN beret and armband in Bosnia has rekindled this debate. One hundred lawmakers have signed a bill to "prevent the President from forcing American soldiers to wear the uniform of the UN."

At root, this controversy hinges upon competing visions of America's military role in the post-cold-war world—whether it should operate largely unilaterally in securing its direct interests, or multilaterally in securing a degree of order in an increasingly fractious world. That is but one of the many courses the commander in chief will have to steer as the violent 20th century draws to a close.

Policy Choices

1. **Defense Budget:**
- ❏ **a.** Maintain defense budget at current level unless there is a significant change in U.S. geopolitical situation.

    OR

- ❏ **b.** Make additional sharp cuts in the defense budget across-the-board and allocate the "peace dividend" to nonmilitary uses.

2. **Defense Spending Priorities:**
- ❏ **a.** Devote relatively scarce Pentagon dollars to maintaining the current preparedness of U.S. forces to wage two major regional conflicts at the same time.

    OR

- ❏ **b.** Allow troop numbers and readiness to decline so as to seize upon the current era of relative peace to invest in the next generation of weapons needed for future potential threats to U.S. interests.

3. **Ballistic Missile Defense:**
- ❏ **a.** Continue stressing the development of tactical missile defense systems against battlefield missiles, while putting research into national defenses on a slow track. Adhere to ABM treaty.

    OR

- ❏ **b.** Move expeditiously to erect a system that can defend the continental U.S. against misfired missiles or those launched by rogue states. Renounce the ABM treaty.

4. **Nuclear Nonproliferation:**
- ❏ **a.** Use nonmilitary means—diplomatic and economic—to reduce the potential nuclear danger emanating from post-Soviet states or aggressively proliferating nations.

    OR

- ❏ **b.** Rely upon traditional nuclear deterrence and missile defenses to forestall any nuclear threat from regimes hostile to the U.S.

5. **Peacekeeping:**
- a. Continue selectively working with the UN and individual governments to combat genocide or the breakdown of civil authority in war-torn lands.

OR

- b. Pursue a military policy that more carefully weighs direct U.S. interests in overseas conflicts and acts accordingly.

Select Bibliography

Center for International Security and Arms Control, Stanford University. Publishes its own series of reports and papers and sponsors *Studies in International Security and Arms Control* (320 Galvez St., Stanford, Calif. 94305-6165).

The Defense Monitor. Published monthly by the Center for Defense Information, 1500 Massachusetts Ave., N.W., Washington, D.C. 20005. Provides current information on major defense issues.

Morrison, David C., "Defense: Redefining U.S. Needs and Priorities." *Great Decisions 1994,* pp. 49–58. New York, Foreign Policy Association, 1994. Overview of the post-cold-war reassessment of military requirements, forces and policies, and related issues.

Perry, William J., *Annual Report to the President and the Congress.* U.S. Department of Defense, Washington, D.C., Mar. 1996. (Available from U.S. Government Printing Office, 732 N. Capitol Street, N.W., Washington, D.C. 20401.) The secretary of defense's annual report on the state of the military and its future defense plans.

11

U.S. Foreign Aid

✔ *Should the U.S. continue to provide foreign aid?*

✔ *What conditions, if any, should the U.S. place on foreign aid?*

✔ *To which countries and for what purposes should U.S. foreign aid be given?*

Basic Facts

- Foreign aid budget for fiscal year (FY) 1996: $12.8 billion; FY 1995: $14.4 billion; FY 1994: $14.4 billion.
- Major recipients: Israel, $3 billion per year; Egypt, $2.1 billion per year; Turkey, $419 million (FY 1995); Russia, $348 million (FY 1995); Greece, $255 million (FY 1995).
- Foreign aid as % of federal budget is slightly less than 1%. U.S. Agency for International Development (USAID) aid as % of federal budget, approximately 0.5%.
- Foreign aid as % of U.S. gross domestic product (GDP): 0.15% (1994). In 1995 the U.S. contributed the second largest amount (after Japan) but the smallest percentage of GDP to foreign aid of the 21 wealthiest countries.

Background

After World War II, the primary goals of U.S. foreign aid were (1) the reconstruction of Europe, (2) containing communism and (3) fostering worldwide economic prosperity. The $13.3 billion Marshall Plan (1948–52) to rebuild Western Europe was the largest American aid program in U.S. history.

After decolonization of the former European empires, the U.S. shifted its foreign aid focus from Europe to the newly independent nations of the developing world. Among the achievements:

- billions of U.S. foreign aid dollars for South Korea and Taiwan in the 1950s and early 1960s helped set the stage for their later economic miracles—South Korea's GNP per capita has grown from $100 three decades ago to $8,500 today; Taiwan's GNP per capita is $12,000.

- a decrease in the average number of children per family, from 6.1 in the mid-1960s to 4.2 today, in the 28 nations with the largest USAID family-planning programs;

- over 3 million lives saved each year as a result of USAID immunization programs.

Multilateral development programs through the UN and its specialized agencies to which the U.S. provides funds have contributed to

- increased average life expectancy in poor countries by one third in the last 30 years;

- extended health services to more than 70% of their populations;

- increased primary-school enrollment to over 80%.

Despite some successes, foreign aid has failed to lift some 1.5 billion people in the poorest countries out of poverty. The 47 least-developed countries, which represent 10% of the world's population, have only 0.1% of world income. Per capita income in these countries in the last two decades has on average declined.

U.S. foreign aid in the past was used predominantly to support U.S. strategic objectives—to reward countries, not necessarily the most needy or the most democratic—that backed the war on communism. Development assistance took second place. Many liberals objected to using aid to prop up authoritarian regimes simply because they were anti-Communist. Many conservatives often complained about "pouring money down ratholes."

After the cold war, in the early 1990s, when U.S. foreign aid could no longer be justified as a weapon in the war on communism, supporters of foreign aid argued that it continued to serve U.S. interests by helping the economy at home, promoting democracy and free-market economies abroad and forestalling or stabilizing crises.

The current debate on the future of foreign aid centers on three issues: the goals, the budget priorities and the organizational structure.

Current Status

Goals

Critics claim that foreign assistance lacks focus and direction and spreads resources too thin. The program is still guided by the Foreign Assistance Act of 1961.

In early 1994, the Clinton Administration sent Congress a restructured, post-cold-war foreign aid budget and policy framework, the Peace, Prosperity and Democracy Act. It outlined six major objectives: (1) promoting U.S. prosperity through trade, investment and employment; (2) building democracy; (3) promoting sustainable development; (4) promoting peace; (5) providing humanitarian assistance; and (6) advancing diplomatic goals.

Critics charged that the Administration had simply repackaged old goals and had set too many priorities based on a flawed strategy for advancing U.S. interests.

Budget

The cutback in foreign aid spending—from a high of $19 billion in 1985 to $14.4 billion in FY 1995—was accompanied by a change in priorities. In the post-cold-war period, this country's old enemies, the former Soviet Union and Eastern Europe, became major aid recipients ($1.2 billion in FY 1995); aid to Africa increased in

1991 and remained at the higher level through FY 1995; environmental and population projects grew, as did disaster and refugee relief.

For FY 1996 President Bill Clinton proposed a $15.2 billion foreign aid budget, a 6% increase over FY 1995. What the President signed in January 1996 fell far short of his request—$12.8 billion. Funding for priority activities on which there was a consensus between the Administration and Congress did not change substantially. These included aid for Egypt and Israel, humanitarian relief and refugees, children's activities and aid

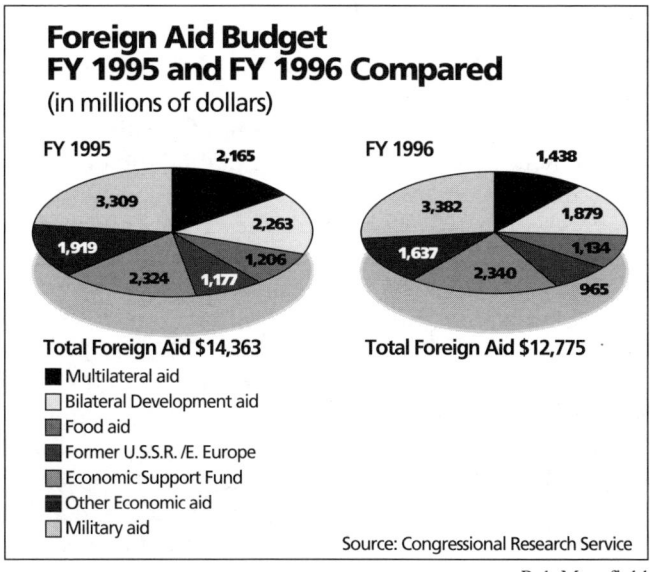

Foreign Aid Budget FY 1995 and FY 1996 Compared
(in millions of dollars)

FY 1995: 2,165; 3,309; 2,263; 1,919; 1,206; 2,324; 1,177
Total Foreign Aid $14,363

FY 1996: 1,438; 3,382; 1,879; 1,637; 1,134; 2,340; 965
Total Foreign Aid $12,775

- Multilateral aid
- Bilateral Development aid
- Food aid
- Former U.S.S.R. /E. Europe
- Economic Support Fund
- Other Economic aid
- Military aid

Source: Congressional Research Service

Bob Mansfield

to Russia (the latter is a high Administration priority, but support in Congress slipped in 1995). But bilateral economic assistance outside the Middle East and Europe fell about 25% below the President's request. The areas most affected by the cuts were Africa, Latin America and Asia, and global population and environmental projects. Multilateral programs, particularly the World Bank's affiliate, the International Development Association, which lends money to the poorest countries, were subjected to cuts as well.

Supporters of foreign aid contend that the cuts are so

deep that they can prevent the U.S. from meeting emergency needs. Critics, on the other hand, contend that more cuts are possible: what is needed is greater selectivity, for example, dropping countries that are economically advanced or that mismanage aid funds.

Organization

Five major government agencies and several other organizations manage some 30 U.S. foreign aid programs in nearly 100 countries. The lead agency is USAID. Since 1993, it has been reorganized and 15 overseas missions have been closed. Nine more are scheduled to close by the end of 1997. Critics maintain that the agency is mismanaged, its programs are ineffective and the reorganization has not gone far enough.

In 1995, Secretary of State Warren Christopher proposed merging USAID and two other independent foreign affairs agencies, the Arms Control and Disarmament Agency (ACDA) and the U.S. Information Agency (USIA), with the State Department, but the White House rejected the idea.

In March 1995, Senate Foreign Relations Committee chairman Jesse A. Helms (R-N.C.) introduced a plan to abolish USAID, along with ACDA and USIA, and distribute its economic aid responsibilities throughout the State Department. Helms said his plan would save $3.6 billion. (When Democrats filibustered Helms's bill, the senator responded by halting consideration of all legislation before the Foreign Relations Committee for four months, including the second strategic arms reduction treaty and 18 ambassadorial nominations.)

An alternative plan would require the President to abolish at least one of the three agencies and certify to Congress that his foreign policy agency reorganization would achieve $1.7 billion in budget savings over four years. The Administration has said it would veto the legislation.

The congressional debate on the organizational proposals raised a number of questions: Is a single aid agency necessary to carry out a consistent and comprehensive bilateral aid strategy? What would be the

Foreign Aid ■ 117

Danziger©*The Christian Science Monitor*

relationship between U.S. economic aid goals and export-trade promotion efforts?

Two of the most contentious issues in the 1996 foreign aid debate were international family planning and abortion restrictions. USAID population assistance was reduced to no more than 65% of the 1995 total.

Public perceptions and misperceptions

In a 1995 opinion poll, 75% of Americans surveyed felt the U.S. was spending too much on foreign aid. When asked how much they thought the U.S. was spending, the answers averaged 18% of the federal budget—more than 18 times the actual level. When informed of the actual spending level, the thinking shifted substantially. While 18% still thought 1% was too much, 33% believed it was "too little," and 46% felt it was "about right."

Policy Choices

1. **The U.S. should reduce or eliminate foreign aid and "fix America first."**
- ❏ **Yes.** Senator Helms and Republican presidential candidate Patrick J. Buchanan want to reduce sharply or eliminate foreign assistance. To quote Buchanan:

"I believe we should [have] ended foreign aid.... We Americans have got to start looking out for our own country and our own people first for a change. I tell [you], to me...that means ending foreign aid, and thinking about the forgotten Americans right here in the United States."

Critics of foreign aid argue that it has not rescued countries from poverty. Of the 34 nations on the conservative Heritage Foundation's list of unfree economies that have received U.S. aid for 35 years or more, 26 are no better off than they were 30 years ago.

❑ **No.** Foreign aid has helped to lift some countries out of dire economic straits, and by laying the groundwork for future market economies and trading partners it creates American jobs and enhances U.S. prosperity. Of the 50 largest buyers of U.S. farm products, according to USAID, 43 once received American foreign aid.

Moreover, foreign assistance improves American national security. Well-designed foreign aid programs can head off future crises which would be far more costly to resolve than to prevent.

2. The U.S. should limit aid to strategically vital countries and regions.

❑ **Yes.** In a time of budget scarcity, the U.S. must further prioritize its foreign aid spending. Only by focusing exclusively on certain countries and regions can the U.S. make a difference with its foreign assistance.

❑ **No.** "You can't pursue the kind of political strategies we have—supporting democracy and trying to develop market systems—if poor nations are constantly at war with their ability to feed people and to provide a decent life and opportunity," notes a senior State Department official.

3. The U.S. should tie strings to its aid.

❑ **Yes.** The U.S. can advance its interests by insisting that potential aid recipients undertake certain measures, including political and economic reforms, to qualify for assistance. Republican presidential hopefuls, former Senate Majority Leader Bob Dole (Kan.) and Senator Richard G. Lugar (Ind.), for example, advocate tying economic assistance to Russia and the other post-Soviet republics to their agreement not to export technology that can be used to build weapons of mass destruction.

- **No.** The U.S. should refrain from interfering in the internal affairs of recipient states. It becomes too tempting for such countries to blame their economic or political problems on the U.S. Developing countries need to be focusing on correcting the causes of such problems.

4. **The U.S. should distribute more of its aid through multilateral agencies.**
- **Yes.** This would distance the U.S. from much of the scapegoating and many of the disagreements that arise from bilateral aid arrangements. It would also enable the U.S. to reduce its foreign aid bureaucracy. Furthermore, multilateral organizations such as the International Development Association implement aid programs more effectively than individual governments.
- **No.** The U.S. has greater influence over recipient countries' policies when it gives aid directly. Also, multilateral organizations such as the UN suffer from bureaucratic bloat and inefficiency.

Select Bibliography

"Beyond Aid." *United Nations Development Program.* New York, United Nations Development Program, Division of Public Affairs, Nov. 1995. UNDP makes the case for UN involvement in development assistance.

"Beyond Band-Aids." *The Economist,* Mar. 23, 1996, pp. 15–16. The weekly newsmagazine makes the case that foreign aid needs to be increasingly channeled through multilateral organizations.

Eberstadt, Nicholas, "U.S. Foreign Aid Policy—A Critique." *Headline Series* No. 293. New York, Foreign

Policy Association, Summer 1990. The author gives a historical overview and critique of U.S. foreign assistance in the post–World War II era.

Johnstone, Craig, "Foreign Policy on the Cheap: You Get What You Pay For." *U.S. Department of State Dispatch*, Oct. 16, 1995, pp. 743–45. In a speech to the Seattle World Affairs Council, a council executive defends the Administration's record on foreign aid and decries efforts to scale back foreign assistance.

"Rethinking Foreign Aid: What Kind? How Much? For Whom?" *Great Decisions 1991*, pp. 43–50. New York, Foreign Policy Association, 1991. A look at U.S. foreign aid policy and a review of various options.

Yeoman, Barry, "Statesmanship vs. Helmsmanship." *The Nation*, Feb. 5, 1996, pp. 11–15. The author presents a critical look at Senator Helms's actions on foreign aid and other aspects of U.S. foreign policy.

Index

A

ABM Treaty 47–48, 49, 50, 106, 110
Africa, aid to 114, 115
aid, multilateral 12, 13, 44, 58, 113, 115, 119
  development assistance 95, 101
  humanitarian 12, 13, 20, 21, 94, 101
Alexander, Lamar 59
Arab-Israeli conflict 63, 65–70
  peace process 63–65, 72
Arafat, Yasir 65, 66
Aristide, Jean-Bertrand 13
arms
  control 47, 63, 95
  embargo 20, 25
  ICBMs 47
  Indo-Pakistani nuclear arms race 108
  missiles 36, 46, 68
  nuclear nonproliferation 40, 46, 50
  nuclear reduction 12, 47
  proliferation 71
  sales 36–37, 71
  weapons of mass destruction 12, 65, 71, 72, 119
Asia 8, 12, 90, 115
Asia-Pacific Economic Cooperation forum (APEC) 90–91
al-Assad, Hafez 69, 72

B

Begin, Menachem 66
biological weapons. See arms, weapons of mass destruction
Belarus 12, 48
Bihac 21
Bosnia and Herzegovina 10, 12, 14, 17–27, 96, 98, 109
  arms embargo 20, 25
  Dayton accords 17, 20, 22–23, 25, 26
  ethnic cleansing 23
  ethnic division 17, 18, 20, 23
  safe areas 21–22
  Sarajevo 20, 21, 22
  Srebrenica 21
  UN hostages 21
  UN peace plans 20–21
Boutros-Ghali, Boutros 95
Britain 24, 94, 95
Buchanan, Patrick J. 38, 59, 87, 117
Bush, George 24, 89, 91, 97, 103, 104

C

Cambodia 95
Camp David 63, 66, 67
Canada 30, 86, 89, 90
capitalism, promoting 8, 10, 40, 44, 114
Carter, Jimmy 66
Chechnya 40, 45–46
Chernomyrdin, Viktor S. 40
Chiang Kai-shek 30
Chile 89, 90, 91
China, People's Republic of (PRC) 7, 28–39, 49, 75, 87, 90, 92, 94
  arms exports 30, 36–37, 71
  constructive engagement 32, 37
  economic growth 30
  human rights 32, 33, 35
  military establishment 8, 28
  nuclear power 30
  Taiwan 35–36
  U.S.-China relations 32–37
Christopher, Warren 70–71, 72, 116
Clinton, Bill 11, 12, 13, 14, 24–

25, 33, 36, 43, 44, 45, 46, 47, 49, 58, 65, 71, 79, 86, 87, 89, 97, 103, 104, 105, 106, 108, 115
  Administration 8, 13, 14, 24–26, 32, 34, 35, 36, 43, 44, 45, 46, 49–50, 57, 58–59, 70–71, 79, 80–81, 88, 89, 90–91, 99–101, 104, 105, 107, 108, 114, 115, 116
Colosio Murrieta, Luis Donaldo 54–55
communism, containment of 8, 63, 113
Congress 14, 25–26, 34, 44, 58, 79–80, 89, 91, 99–101, 104, 105, 106, 107, 114, 115, 116–7
Contract with America 105
Croatia 17, 19, 20, 22, 23

D

Dayton accords 17, 20, 22–23, 25, 26
defense 103–111
  ballistic missile defense (BMD) 11, 47, 49, 50, 103, 104, 106–7, 110
  base force 10–12, 104–5
  budget 11, 104
  Bottom-Up Review (BUR) 104–105
  funding cuts 103
  modernization procurement 104, 105
  nuclear proliferation 104
  nuclear stockpiles, dismantling 104, 107
  Star Wars 106
  troops 11–12, 23, 24–25, 104, 105
DeLay, Tom 101
democracy, promoting 8, 40, 44, 114
Deng Xiaoping 29–30
Dole, Bob 11, 12, 13, 14, 25, 33, 44, 47–48, 49, 59, 78, 87, 89, 101, 119
domestic issues 10
Doolittle, John 101
drug traffic 56–57, 60, 96

E

economy 10, 56, 84–93
  jobs in U.S. 13, 34, 56, 59–60, 77, 81, 84, 85–87, 90, 91, 92
  unemployment 84
  wages 77, 81, 84, 85–87, 92
Egypt 63, 66, 112, 115
Europe 8, 11–12, 18, 49, 71, 86, 103, 113, 115
European Community 20
European Union (EU) 24, 88–89

F

family-planning programs 113, 117
Forbes, Steve 59
foreign aid, U.S. 8, 10, 13, 14, 15, 44, 47, 49, 50, 57, 63, 66, 70, 112–120
  budget 112, 114–6
  children's 115
  cuts to 10
  development assistance 114
  disaster relief 115
  environmental aid 115
  family-planning programs 113, 117
  Foreign Assistance Act of 1961 114
  goals 114
  humanitarian assistance 114, 115
  Marshall Plan 113
  multilateral programs 115, 119
  organization 116–7
  population projects 115
  popular perceptions of aid 117
  refugee relief 115
  State Department 116
France 24, 94, 95
Freedom Support Act 44

G

Gaza Strip 63, 66, 68
General Agreement on Tariffs and Trade (GATT) 12, 85, 87

Germany 23
Golan Heights 63, 66, 69
Goldstone, Richard 23
Gorbachev, Mikhail S. 41, 45
Gore, Al 25
Gramm, Phil 25–26
Greece 112
Group of Seven (G-7) 10

H

Haiti 12, 13, 108
Hamilton, Lee 32
Helms, Jesse A. 116, 117
Hezbollah 68, 70
Holbrooke, Richard C. 22
Hong Kong 28, 29, 32, 37
   U.S.–Hong Kong Policy Act 37
human rights 32, 35, 50, 60
   linked to aid 50
   linked to trade 32, 38
Hussein, Saddam 65, 72

I

IFOR (Implementation Force) 23, 25
immigration 10, 56, 57–58, 59, 60, 74–83
   amnesty 76–77
   Bracero Program 75
   Chinese Exclusion Acts 75
   employer sanctions 77, 79, 82
   family reunification 75, 77, 79–80, 81
   Immigration Reform and Control Act (IRCA) 76–77
   lottery 76
   McCarran-Walter Immigration and Nationality Act of 1952 75
   National Origins Quota Act of 1924 75
   public services for immigrants 77, 82–83
   quota reductions 79, 81
   Refugee Act of 1980 76
   refugees 75, 77
   Special Agricultural Worker (SAW) 76–77
INS. See U.S. Immigration and Naturalization Service.
intellectual property rights 34
   copyrights 34
   piracy 34
   trademarks 34
International Monetary Fund (IMF) 44, 58
International War Crimes Tribunal 23, 26
intifada 66, 67
Iran 12, 21, 36, 49, 63, 65, 71, 72–73, 108
   defense budget 62
   Iran-Iraq war 65
   nuclear capabilities 49, 65
   oil 63, 65
   trade embargo 62, 71, 72–73
Iraq 63, 71, 72, 95, 108
   defense budget 62
   Iran-Iraq war 65
   Kuwait 65
   oil 63, 65
   UN sanctions 65, 72
Israel 62–73
   defense budget 62
   Labor party 68, 71
   Likud 62, 67, 68, 69, 72
   nuclear power 65
   occupied territories 63
   Oslo negotiations 67
   peace process 67–69
   Security Council Resolution 242 66
   security zone 66
   Syrian relations 69–70
   "territory for peace" 66, 69, 72
   U.S. foreign aid to 63, 112, 115

J

Japan 7, 11, 30, 49, 71, 73, 86, 90, 92, 95, 108, 112
Jerusalem 63, 66, 69
Jiang Zemin 30
Jordan 66

K

Kantor, Mickey 34
Karadzic, Radovan 18, 20, 22, 23, 24

Kassebaum, Nancy 99
Krajina 22
Kuril Islands 48
Kuwait 65, 95

L

Latin America 90, 92, 115
Lebanon 66, 68, 70
Lee Teng-hui 30–31, 35
Lugar, Richard G. 119

M

Macedonia 12, 19
Madrid Conference 67, 69
Mao Zedong 29
McCain, John 25
Mexico 52–61, 89, 92
   Chiapas 54–55
   Declaration of the Lacondona Jungle 54
   economic growth 53, 55
   financial crisis 55, 56, 58, 89, 92
   immigration, illegal 57–58, 59
   Institutional Revolutionary Party (PRI) 53, 55
   political instability 54–55
   reforms 53–54
   Zapatista National Liberation Army (EZLN) 54–55
Middle East 10, 12, 14, 62–73, 75–76, 115
   Arab-Israeli conflict 63, 65–70
   Palestinian state 68, 69, 71
   Summit of the Peacemakers 68
   See also individual countries
migrant workers 57–58, 60
military
   establishment 7, 8, 9
   funding 14
   intelligence 24
   See also defense
Milosevic, Slobodan 18, 22
Mladic, Ratko 21, 23, 24
Montenegro 19, 22
most-favored-nation (MFN) status 33–34, 37

N

Netanyahu, Benjamin 68–69, 72
Nicaragua 56
nonproliferation. See arms control.
North American Free Trade Agreement (Nafta) 13, 52, 56, 59, 84, 89, 91, 92
North Atlantic Treaty Organization (NATO) 8, 10, 14, 17, 21–22, 23, 24, 26, 41, 48–49, 50
   expansion 48–49
   IFOR 23, 25
North Korea 103, 107, 108
Nuclear Nonproliferation Treaty (NPT) 12, 36, 65
nuclear capabilities 8, 30, 36–37, 65, 71, 108
   arsenals 46
   comprehensive test ban 36–37
   weapons proliferation 12, 65, 71
nuclear environmental cleanup 107
nuclear compliance 107
Nunn-Lugar assistance (Cooperative Threat Reduction) 47, 107

O

oil 63, 65
Organization of American States (OAS) 53
Oslo negotiations 67
   Declaration of Principles on Interim Self-Government and Arrangements 67

P

Pakistan 12, 36
Palestine Liberation Organization (PLO) 65, 66–69, 72
Palestinian Authority (PA) 67–68, 70
Partnership for Peace Program 41
peacekeeping 66, 103, 104, 108–9, 111

U.S. forces 12, 18, 23, 24–25, 66
Pelosi, Nancy 36
Peres, Shimon 68, 69, 71
Perry, William J. 24, 106
Persian Gulf 11, 24, 63, 65, 67, 71
Pressler, Larry 99
Proposition 187 58, 77

R

Rabin, Yitzhak 65, 67, 68
Reagan, Ronald 97, 106
refugees 8, 18, 20, 22, 23, 66, 68, 75, 77, 96, 97–98
Russia 8, 12, 40–51, 71, 95, 107, 112, 115, 119
 aid 47, 49, 50
 Black Sea Fleet 48
 Chechnya 40, 45–46
 Communist resurgence 40, 41, 43, 45, 49
 defense spending 41
 dismantling nuclear stockpiles 12
 economic reform 40, 41, 43–44, 49, 50
 foreign relations 48–49
 military 40, 45–48, 50
 nuclear weapons control 46, 47, 50
 parliament 41, 44, 45, 47
 political reform 41, 44–45, 49, 50
 See also Soviet Union
Rwanda 12, 96, 108

S

al-Sadat, Anwar 66
safe areas 21–22
Salinas de Gortari, Carlos 53–54, 55, 58
sanctions
 UN 22, 24–25, 62, 65, 71, 72
 unilateral 34, 36
Sandinistas 56
Sarajevo 20, 21, 22
Sasser, James 35
Saudi Arabia 21, 63
Scarborough, Joe 101
Serbia 17, 18, 20, 22

Slovenia 19
Somalia 10, 12, 96
South Korea 108, 113
Soviet Union 8, 10, 41, 45, 47, 48, 50, 107, 114
 collapse of 9, 43, 45, 48, 63
Specter, Arlen 36
Summit of the Americas 90
strategic arms reduction treaties (Start, Start II) 41, 46–47, 107
Syria 62, 66, 68, 69–70, 72
 defense budget 62
 Golan Heights 66, 69
 Israeli relations 69–70
 terrorism 68, 69, 70, 72

T

Taiwan 28, 29, 30–32, 35–36, 38, 49, 113
 China, Republic of (ROC) 30, 32
 economic growth 31
 reunification with China 32
 Taiwan Relations Act of 1979 32
Taylor, Morry 59
terrorism 12, 63, 67, 68–69, 70, 71, 72, 95
Tiananmen Square 30, 35
Tito, Josip Broz 19
trade 33–35, 53, 56, 84–93
 barriers 34–35, 56, 85, 92
 blocs 88–90
 deficit 84, 89
 free trade 7, 10, 12–13, 15, 59, 84, 85, 88–90
 global 8, 14
 MFN status 33–34, 37
 multilateralism vs. bilateralism 87–88, 91
 protectionism 12–13, 85, 91
 sanctions 34, 36, 56, 71, 72, 91
 subsidies 89
Tudjman, Franjo 18

U

Ukraine 12, 48
United Nations 8, 10, 13, 17, 21, 23, 31, 53, 65, 66, 94–102

arrears 99
assessed dues 95, 99
budget 95, 98, 99–101
development assistance 95, 101
General Assembly 94, 99
human rights 95
Human Rights Commission 35
humanitarian emergencies 97–98, 101
International War Crimes Tribunal 23–24, 26
Kassebaum Amendment 99
management reform 97, 98–99, 101
military observer forces 96
mismanagement 98–99
Office of Internal Oversight 99
peacekeeping 21, 25–26, 66, 94, 95, 96–98, 99, 101
Pressler Amendment 99
refugees 96, 97–98
sanctions 20, 21, 22, 24–25, 62, 65, 71, 72
Secretariat 94, 99, 100
Security Council 23, 72, 94
Unprofor 21, 24
U.S. Agency for International Development (USAID) 112, 113, 116–7, 118
U.S. Immigration and Naturalization Service (INS) 58, 59
U.S. leadership role 7, 9–10, 13–14

W

war crimes 21, 23–24, 26
West Bank 63, 66, 68, 69, 70
Wiesel, Elie 69
Wilson, Pete 79
World Bank 18, 44, 95, 115
 International Development Association 115
World Trade Organization (WTO) 35, 38, 87–88, 91

Y

Yeltsin, Boris 40, 43, 44, 45, 46, 49, 50

Yugoslavia 17, 18–20, 23, 24, 95, 108

Z

Zedillo Ponce de León, Ernesto 53, 54, 58
Zhirinovsky, Vladimir 49
Zyuganov, Gennadi 40, 43

FPA invites you...
to send for current reading materials guaranteed to help you—your associates—your students—keep pace with world events

GREAT DECISIONS

Prepared annually by FPA's editors, this 96-page briefing book contains
- background on eight critical international issues facing the U.S.
- impartial review of the pros and cons of current U.S. policy
- discussion questions and bibliographies
- opinion ballots
- maps, charts and cartoons
- a free color **WORLD MAP**

$12.00

Lively and provocative, the quarterly issues are written by experts and cover current problems and critical areas of the world. Recent issues of this concise (usually 64 pages) and readable publication:

"Hong Kong and China: 'One Country, Two Systems'?" (HS 310) *by Frank Ching*

"Microbes Versus Mankind: The Coming Plague" (HS 309) *by Laurie Garrett*

"U.S. Information Policy and Cultural Diplomacy" (HS 308) *by Frank Ninkovich*

"The Status of Women in Foreign Policy" (HS 307) *by Nancy E. McGlen & Meredith Reid Sarkees*

"Divided Korea: United Future?" (HS 306) *by Bruce Cumings*

HEADLINE SERIES

Subscribe to the *Headline Series:*
$20 for 4 issues;
$35 for 8 issues;
$50 for 12 issues.

Individual copies, $5.95

Double issues, $11.25

FPA SPECIALS... In addition to the quadrennial *Citizen's Guide to U.S. Foreign Policy Issues* ($9.95), FPA publishes a best-selling *Guide to Careers in World Affairs* (3d ed., 442 pp., $14.95) and *A Cartoon History of U.S. Foreign Policy From 1945 to the Present* (239 pp., $12.95).

ORDER FORM

PLEASE MAIL TO: Foreign Policy Association
Sales and Circulation
470 Park Avenue South
New York, N.Y. 10016-6819

FAX: (212) 481-9275 **OR CALL TOLL-FREE:** (800) 477-5836

SHIP TO: (PLEASE PRINT)

Name _____

Address _____

City _____ State _____ Zip _____

Daytime phone (with area code) _____

PLEASE SEND ME:
- ❏ a free FPA publications catalogue
- ❏ a free color World Map

HOW MANY	TITLE	PRICE EACH	TOTAL
	Total price of items		
	Shipping and handling*		
NY state residents, please add 8.25% sales tax			
	Total cost		

- Discounts on 10 or more copies.
- Prepayment must accompany all orders from individuals.

*SHIPPING AND HANDLING

Headline Series: $2.50 for first copy, 50¢ for each additional copy. All other publications: $3.00 for first copy, 50¢ for each additional copy.

METHOD OF PAYMENT
- ❏ Check enclosed (payable to Foreign Policy Association)
- ❏ Purchase order attached
- ❏ American Express   ❏ Visa   ❏ Mastercard

Credit Card # _____

Expiration date _____ Signature _____